JUST ADD A ZERO

Remove the Film, Outperform your
Competition, and Grow Exponentially
through Collaboration

JUST ADD A ZERO

Remove the Film, Outperform your
Competition, and Grow Exponentially
through Collaboration

Chad T. Jenkins

ethos
collective

Dedication

This book is dedicated to those who make it possible for me to be me - my lovely wife Jennifer, and my two beautiful daughters, Adelaide and Carson. Without your love, patience and support none of this could be possible.

Contents

Introduction

C ONSIDER THE WINDSHIELD IN your car on a crisp fall morning. The dew is thick—not quite frost. You could get in and put the car in drive; however, it might be a bit dangerous. Windshield wipers, defrosters, and a little elbow grease make things a bit safer.

That protector the electronics industry puts on every device works the same way. Except that sometimes you don't even know it's there for a while. The television doesn't have as much definition as it did in the store. Your alarm clock seems to collect dirt and eventually you can't get it clean. Why does the gaming console have a bubble in the cover? Then, a corner of the thin plastic pops up and a whole new world lies in front of you as you pull back the film.

Unfortunately, too many people have left the film on their business and their life. They don't ask why things are blurry or even try to pull that tab to see the potential quantum leap opportunities that lie beneath to create value. When trouble hits, instead of getting rid of the fog that confuses their vision, they maintain the status quo or back track. Zeros can't grow in the garden of complacency.

One of my favorite accomplishments has been peeling back the film on existing business models to reveal true, innovative solutions and collaborations for myself and entrepreneurs; I simply can't help it. Removing the film has helped me start and grow over thirty-five businesses. Some say it's one of the secrets to my success. Though many of the attributes that have led me down this path have been part of my nature since birth or instilled in me by my upbringing, most can be learned and replicated. I feel blessed to be able to help other entrepreneurs become Friction Identifiers who Leverage the Market—a much more productive and exciting kind of FILM that begs to be removed in most businesses and even some industries, though most do not see it.

The thought process necessary to Just Add a Zero has inspired the core values of all my companies. While other businesses have unilateral core values, ours build upon one another. They create a flywheel effect like Jim Collins describes in his book *Good to Great.* Every associate in our circle has their mind fixed to constantly pursue the why, maintain perspective, take ownership, and share the win—all for the benefit of creating true value for others—the type of value you feel when you open a new product from Apple®. And the result is JAAZ—Just Add a Zero.

Before we can truly take the steps necessary to add zeros, we must train ourselves to see the opportunities. Until we learn to identify the often-invisible connections and what could really be made of them, we won't move in the direction of natural curiosity. But when we do, clarity will come, and you'll see that success is as easy as Just Adding a Zero to what is already there but invisible to most.

Part One: Confusion

CHAPTER 1

Learning to See Through the Film

If you can sniff out suffering, you can sniff out problems, and if you can solve those problems, there is no limit to what you can accomplish.

—Joe Polish

F IVE BLIND MEN ENTER a room, and someone leads them to stand in five different places around an elephant. Never having been told about a beast so mighty before, each one is asked to tell the group what is in the room based on what they feel. One describes a long rough rope thicker than any he'd ever felt before. The second tells the group that the first man is mistaken, the rope is quite thin and frayed at the end. A third man tells the others that the object is more like a pillar than a rope, quite sturdy, it will hold a massive amount of weight, while the fourth describes a holding tank. "It might be excellent for water storage," the blind man remarks. The fifth had a difficult time keeping hold of the part he stood closest too. "It flutters around," he says, "I couldn't really grasp it, but the little I touched felt like a thick piece of leather ready to be made into a coat. It must be a piece of leather cloth on a clothesline."

All five described their area accurately; however, none were correct, and all remained quite confused because they didn't have the full picture.

Many individuals and businesses today exist in a similar state of cloudiness and confusion about what real opportunity exists for them. They see only their little piece of the world and they evaluate it based on things they know. The fact something new might be standing right in front of them never crosses their mind, and they miss the magnitude of what might be possible if they took what they can see and melded it with another's vision. Though limitless potential lies right outside the door, most never venture beyond the walls of the familiar.

Caught Up in Convention

One thief of added zeros is the Seven Deadly Words—*We have always done it that way.* This phrase has killed countless movements, churches, and civic groups. Unfortunately, life gives no exemptions for businesses. When entrepreneurs get stuck in conventional value creation, growth can't happen. Even individuals extremely capable of something great can get caught in the mindset of my *family's always done it that way.*

By the time we hit our teens, nearly every person has decided, "I will not become my mother—or father—when I grow up." Two decades later, we realize the unthinkable happened, there in the mirror we see the gestures, hear the words, and wonder how in the world this transpired.

I was fortunate to have grown up on a farm with a wonderful family, and while I love the outdoors and having a lot of space for living, it didn't take long for me to figure out I was not cut out for manually digging post holes and stringing barbed wire sixty hours a week. Though I wouldn't trade the work ethic and integrity instilled in me from my parents for anything in the world, I quickly began creating a set of methods that empowered me to create my own path.

In his autobiography, Teddy Roosevelt quoted Squire Bill Widener who said, "Do what you can, with what you have, where you are." I took this to heart. My early realization that farm living was not the life for me helped me escape the *we have always done it that way* career mentality.

Unfortunately, too many folks find themselves caught up in a conventional existence. They see what worked for their family, and they follow that path because it seems to set them up for success. Plus, let's face it, the familiar is comfortable. Family legacies, tremendous parents we don't want to let down, and fulfilling a dream someone else fashioned all lead to people living less than their best.

Others get stuck in their hometown or college allegiances. They choose their university based on alumni scholarships, then feel obligated to live up to a degree that took a big chunk of time and money to complete. Conventional thinking pushes them into respectable careers and keeps them from looking beyond traditional arenas.

Entrepreneurs in small- to medium-sized businesses get caught on the hamster wheel of conventional thinking. Owners think they can't afford to hire new employees, or the person who could do the job the best wants ten thousand more a year than they budgeted. Those same entrepreneurs think they can run every aspect of the business. They end up working long hours with a lot less productivity than if they had hired the new guy because they don't do it as well as a new person could. How do I know? I used to be that guy. In the first few businesses I started, I worked much more than I should have, and after I began to focus on bringing talented people on staff, I saw how much better and more efficient someone gifted in that area could be. Fortunately, I'm not that guy anymore. I've learned my lesson.

Using Blinders the Right Way

You may have heard the phrase, "They have blinders on." But if you've never been on a farm, you may not understand their true purpose. Owners give racehorses blinders so they can't see the competition or get distracted by the crowd. Draft horses that pull plows and wagons don them for much the same reason. If they see the fun going on around them, they will lose their focus. At the track, blinders can mean the difference between first and last place.

Take the 2016 Summer Olympics for example. Chad LeClos, the swimming champion from South Africa came out on top of Michael Phelps in at least one of the medals, but when he chose to focus on Phelps rather than the finish line in the two-hundred meter butterfly—a race he'd taken from Phelps on two previous occasions—he lost. Perhaps if the star athlete had used blinders so he couldn't see Phelps, he could have focused on the finish line.

I also use blinders; however, I put them on to avoid getting distracted by current conventions. I don't want to be bound to the normal approach to solutions. I've found that when I use blinders, like the blinders on the horses, I keep focused on potential opportunities that many others do not see.

Sadly, much of the world has chosen to wear them to block friction. They believe the old adage "ignorance is bliss." The previously unheard-of possibilities make them nervous. They've grown so comfortable with their little piece of the elephant; they don't want to see the magnificent power available if they could imagine the entire beast. Blinders eliminate the possibility of outside perspective, and the wearer becomes so intent on not upsetting the wagon, they can't see any road except the one that's been walked for so long it's really more of a rut than a path.

Blinder folk are like the British Parliament in 1878 calling Edison's new electric lights "unworthy of the attention of practical or scientific men" and Ferdinand Folk who in 1911 said that airplanes were "interesting scientific toys."[1] Those comments seem ludicrous today, but much of the world insists on maintaining this kind of mindset when it comes to anything new. Uber was called a rogue taxi company in 2009, and AirBnB started with three guys renting out an air mattress in their apartment. It's easy to find fault with innovations that fall outside of convention. But when we look at the success of these unlikely endeavors, it should make us think again.

Small business owners as well as those in the corporate world can find themselves dismissing lucrative ideas to create unconventional value if they forget to pursue why and maintain perspective. The world is changing faster than most can handle. Fixation on what worked two years ago, over cautious budgeting, and fear of someone stealing ideas kills twenty-first century growth. In his book *Blockchain Life*, Kary Oberbrunner points out that over the past four decades, the way the world operates has morphed.[2] With the advance of the internet and technology, our grandparents' mentality of self-sufficiency bringing success has moved through an attitude of competition and into the realm of collaboration. More and more people are beginning to understand there is a clear path to 1+1=5.

Unfortunately, collaboration scares small business owners, corporate executives, and even most individuals. Who can

I trust? I've always managed on my own before, why do I need someone else now? Moving into this arena of unconventional thinking goes against the grain of folks who've been traveling down the same path for decades.

Every company begins with fresh hopes and dreams. But too often, they start with a very traditional methodology. Let's come up with a product, print flyers, take out ads, do some digital marketing, and copy the strategy of the guy down the street. The typical start-up hopes it can beat the competition on price, quality, or customer service.

As the enterprise grows, one of two things happens: either the owner becomes so busy he, or she doesn't have time to be creative anymore or the company grows to the point a board of directors out of touch with the core values takes over. In both cases, productive change becomes non-existent. Innovation gets caught in the wheels of busyness, and if modifications happen to occur, they're random or change for the sake of change rather than growth based on curiosity about what could be.

The biggest problem is that the owners aren't doing anything different. Many businesses become successful with a conventional mindset. They're happy with 2-10 percent growth each year. But what if you could add a zero to that thinking?

I want more for companies and individuals than a boring, conventional, single zero existence. But too few aren't naturally wired to think this way and until now there wasn't a go to guide that empowers them to break the mold.

Running from Friction

Ingenuity, originality, and constant adaptations drive successful businesses. Whether it's an entrepreneur or someone entering the job market, most don't seem to mind the extra work a new endeavor requires. At some point, though, the rough road gets old. After a few years, shouldn't it be smooth sailing?

Sadly, like any road, even if it's smooth for a while, after it's been traveled repeatedly, bumps and divots appear. Irritation bubbles when everyone sidesteps the potholes rather than fixing them.

I suppose if the stress was as obvious as a street that needs paved, someone might jump in to do something about it. But in business, the annoyance is more like an oil leak in a car. When the lubricant gets low, the metal parts create friction. The driver who appreciates a finely tuned vehicle takes care of the problem immediately. Others, those who focus on the funds required to fix the leak or prefer to pretend the problem doesn't exist, simply turn up the radio so they can't hear the tell-tale symptoms.

Likewise, those who notice friction in a business have two options. They can either work on a solution or close the blinds, so they don't have to see or hear the chaos. Unfortunately, if you choose option two, friction still controls the situation. You can choose to embrace it or wait until it forces you to act. Your choice will determine whether you have exponential success or merely a modicum of progress despite the missed opportunity.

It's important to further understand that like oil in the car, even silencing the friction in the most efficient manner possible won't stop the irritation forever. In fact, the most successful entrepreneurs will testify that the cure for friction always causes new friction, and those who live in fear of the discomfort would rather turn up the radio, put on those blinders, and walk the other way.

Most assume any kind of pain must have negative roots, but friction arises from a variety of places. Some obvious culprits are infighting, abused employees, supply chain issues, cash flow turns, undervalued staff, and a lack of organization. But at least as much friction comes from new technology, industry changes and shifts, welcoming innovative staff, and upscaling. We need to remember that beauty and enjoyment follow the spark created by controlled friction.

Consider handblown glass or refined gold. Both require the heat of a red-hot fire to reach perfection. Even sausages cooked over hot coals in a warm house in the Arctic are the result of someone putting a little bit of friction to good use. Some, however, refuse to see the good that can come from the flame.

I love to emphasize the fact that friction produces light. In fact, it's that idea of triboluminescence that forms the name of my company, SeedSpark. When we allow friction to be the seed for light and the spark for creativity, amazing things happen.

One organization I see creating triboluminescence in today's world is BDA, the Biotechnology for Sustainable Development in Africa Foundation. This group, under the leadership of Carole Robert, saw friction in Africa. Millions of people on that continent have been subjected to the life of a nomad. BDA gives these people business skills and helps them own the land. They become farmers who raise African botanicals. BDA creates triboluminescence in the lives of the people of Africa by providing avenues for "trade, not aid." When they introduced me to the organization and to Carole, I could immediately see the light they were creating from the friction.

Good friction in the workplace usually signifies growth. As the business begins to expand, managers will have differing ideas on how to handle the workload. More customers mean service representatives work more hours than they'd like for a time. Storage becomes a problem, mechanical breakdowns happen more often, and fuses can grow short as humans with emotions and personalities have to deal with all the change. Larger companies move from having marvelous ideas inspired by friction identification to ignoring the friction and using every resource to protect their entity. Will you choose to run from the friction or embrace it, put on blinders, or investigate every avenue?

Those who run or wear blinders to the real opportunities that exist never add zeros. Their conventional thinking forces them into the ruts. And when they have to face friction, the blinder crowd prefers noise over change. Little do they know that ignoring the friction doesn't make anything disappear, except perhaps one or even more of those potential zeros.

Blinded by Fear and Excuses

Many times, the blinders of convention have been strapped on by the mere thought of competition. The individuals most blinded will pat themselves on the back for their wisdom. They have used all means possible to shut out their competitors. However, in nearly every case, if they honestly looked at the bigger picture, they would see fear kept them in a foxhole when there wasn't even a battle being waged around them.

The competition mindset is the enemy of adding a zero. Rather than looking for opportunities, the competition mentality scours the horizon for adversaries. Consumed by fear, it hoards resources and stifles growth. This mindset says, "I don't want to lose what I have." What they don't realize is they are losing it little-by-little by holding on so tightly.

Anytime we give our emotions permission to take the wheel, we'll act irrationally. And fear is a strong emotion. Perhaps you've been that person who nearly crashed his car when a spider fell from the visor or stepped on the pointed side of the rake when she saw a snake. You might think those scenarios have nothing to do with careers and business; however, when we sanction an emotion-based reality, the result will be just as dangerous.

Fear feeds negativity. It looks at life like a card game and calls the hand good or bad before the bidding begins. Fear also fuels excuses. Every perceived afront—someone else did something to me—causes pessimism to grow. A common narrative develops among the blinder-fellowship. "We can't because . . ." "I would, but . . ." "I meant to; however, . . ." and one of my favorites, "It's not my fault." The more a person allows their thoughts to travel down the paths of excuses and trepidation, the more fear and negativity grow.

Since the early 1900s, scientists have studied the way the brain processes information. The Institute for Human Optimization shares that "the human brain is constantly evolving, not just through time, but through our own lifetimes. The brain you're born with is not the brain you end up with." The author of the article goes on to say, "The same systems that re-organize your brain to crave exercise can also create negative thought patterns and habits that wreak havoc on your life. Constantly thinking negatively about yourself creates a neuron pathway for this behavior.

The more you engage in negative self-talk, the deeper that pathway runs, the neurons that 'fire together, wire together,' and it becomes a habit."[3]

One hundred years' worth of studies tell us that it doesn't take long for our minds to begin to believe our own excuses and negative talk. Every fearful conclusion or excuse literally creates pathways in our brain that convince us our thoughts are valid. They give us permission to make the next excuse or avoid future friction. Negative firing neurons take over and hatch more negative firing brain cells until we can't see opportunities because they're hidden behind all the reasons we could never move forward. Fear begets fear, and a fear-filled brain cannot add zeros.

Restoring the Art of Collaboration

Humans began collaborating at the dawn of civilization. Early hunter gatherers began experimenting with seeds to produce plants with greater nutritional yield. Native Americans share stories of how their ancestors protected the wild animals so the animals would provide meat for their tribes. Lyricists found composers; poets searched for artists.

The acronym for Just Add a Zero is JAAZ, and jazz music is a tremendous example of the Just Add a Zero philosophy. Unlike symphonic compositions with their consistent, predictable scores and occasional extemporaneous solos, jazz musicians constantly look for ways to improve upon the harmonies. Even the melody line is fair game when a soloist takes their turn. The riffs and occasional discord have given the genre a distinct sound, and only small sections of the improvs are ever reproduced.

Most musicians give us the perfect picture of collaboration. Only those in orchestras and marching bands compete for parts and seats. The rest of the musical world turns those competitors into collaborators. Jazz ensembles, blues bands, bluegrass players, and more invite even amateur musicians to sit in. They understand that each instrument adding its unique sound along with the musicians' ability to hear notes not written creates new beautiful arrangements and one-of-a-kind compositions.

Working together to create something better isn't a new concept, but it's one that began to wane as greed and lack of trust crept in. With the emergence of the industrial revolution, trust levels deteriorated further. Machines began replacing humans, inventors started securing patents to avoid having their ideas stolen, and individuals decided to become more self-sufficient. Two centuries later, even the front porch mentality of the early 1900s has nearly disappeared.

As the world shrinks and costs rise, those who want to thrive have discovered it's time to restore the art of working together. But this requires a reset of those neuron transmitters. We have to rewire the scarcity mindset and turn it into an abundance mentality. Entrepreneurs who want to succeed must begin to reevaluate their territorial fears. People who add zeros know that these fears and excuses for avoiding collaboration make for small-ball thinking.

I love to help companies and individuals move into the big leagues. In the minor leagues, Single-A thinkers watch the competition pass them by. A major league mindset asks, "How can I fix the friction and then add a zero by helping my competition fix the same friction?" The Single-A mentality focuses on hiding their customer list and masking intellectual property. Major leaguers know that spending energy worrying about things like that wears away at their margins. These pro-ball thinkers understand that the Single-A processes aimed at keeping a tight hold chokes profits and washes away opportunity little by little like small waves licking sandstones.

Better Is Infinite

Over the next few chapters, I hope to open your eyes to another perspective about how you and your business or businesses can run more effectively and win in the twenty-first century. Perhaps you'll discover ways life in general can benefit from the Add a Zero mindset. One of the greatest myths that Just Adding A Zero breaks is the concept of limits. People who believe that

> HERE'S THE TRUTH: IT'S NOT HOW SMART YOU ARE; IT'S HOW YOU ARE SMART.
> JIM KWIK

customer lists, ideas, and numbers have maximum capacities begin to hoard their assets and ideas like grain in the middle of a worldwide drought. Limits don't allow us to share or expand. They keep us in boxes.

Businesses miss the zeros when they refuse to see the possibilities available if they'd just take off the blinders. Individuals find themselves stuck when they start to think their ideas will never be heard or they've already reached their maximum earning potential. But what if you could add a zero to any and every aspect of your life?

Narrow-minded thinking limits added zeros to the realm of finances; however, when you apply the JAAZ methodology to your health or time, the quality of your relationships, the way you do business, the reach of your non-profit, the number of people you serve, or any area you can imagine, you'll find the sky is the limit.

Unfortunately, though the possibilities truly are endless, the adages have become so cliché no one believes them anymore. So, let me give you a new phrase—better is infinite.

You see, I'm not what you would call a "better way" guy. I'm a "way better way" guy. This ideology underpins my company, SeedSpark. I could create a solution that makes things better. But why would I do that if I could make it a quantum leap better? Every time we solve a problem, it creates ripples. A great solution will be felt throughout the entire organization. While one area celebrates the success, other areas feel the impact. And sometimes, those feeling the repercussions don't consider them positive. The friction created by whatever made things better in the first area presents an opportunity to make something else greater. It's a never-ending spiral with exciting implications if you're willing to take the leap. Everything you create, everything you learn, can catapult you into something else better. In my case, it's added a couple dozen other businesses to the SeedSpark umbrella.

I've discovered I'm wired a bit differently than most. I see unique patterns and trends and instantaneously connect in unconventional ways to create exponential outcomes. One of my highly respected friends, Lee Brower, often says that while I hear the same things others hear, I see things no one else does. Never do I accomplish a task and say, "Well, that's done." Variables that I can't control abound. I may have resolved an issue for the moment, but things are constantly in motion all around the world. Someone in Hong Kong has a product innovation, and now my solution can create even more value when combined with the mindset to see that as a possible collaboration. New things will always be created that allow me to take "better" to "exceptional."

Don't worry, I understand that not everyone visualizes things the way I do. Sometimes I think I'm a little crazy because of the way I process information to create value. But I love sharing the JAAZ framework with those who want to leap forward but don't have a dominant occipital lobe like mine. Almost anyone can learn to use natural curiosity to their advantage if they are willing to adjust their mindset.

Additionally, I believe everyone on the planet has genius inside of them. You may not do physics or solve string theory, but genius is not limited to science and math labs. Over the years, I've analyzed the way my brain works and used the process to create my own flywheel of, as Jim Collins puts it, "proven methodologies for unconventional thinking that leads to unconventional results."[4] I want to help you discover your genius by sharing SeedSpark's Flywheel. When you learn to remove the FILM, Just Add a Zero, and create Growth through Collaboration, you will be unstoppable.

It's time to remove the film of convention through Friction Identification and Leveraging the Market (FILM). The riffs we create as we add new notes to life may cause discord for just a moment, but the result will be as wonderful as a sonata that's never been heard before. Let's journey together as we examine your past, present, and future from a different perspective to take off the blinders, move out of a conventional existence, and start adding zeros to all your endeavors.

Part Two: Curiosity

CHAPTER 2

Pursue the Why

The one real object of education is to leave a person in the condition of continually asking questions.

—Bishop Mandell Crieghton

I COULDN'T HAVE BEEN more than nine when I realized roughly how much money my father made that year. My brain immediately began to do the reverse math, by month, by week, and by day. . . By the time I took it back to his hourly wage, I thought, *there's no way anyone will ever pay me that much.* Without even realizing it, I started looking into the future—wondering, planning, and pushing my curiosity into overdrive. *What can I do to make as much as my dad? What do I have that I can use to create value for others?* Though I didn't understand economics or paychecks, I realized my father must be providing some serious sort of value to the people who paid him for his time. It scared me to think I might need to make that much to live, and what if I wanted to do more? I started to consider what kind of value I'd need to bring if I wanted to add a zero to my father's annual earnings. I figured if I wanted to make that kind of money, I'd have to learn to create immense value too. And though I didn't know it at the time, Just Add a Zero was born.

From that moment on, my internal wiring began searching for ways to add exponential value to businesses, processes, and even products. Each time I found a problem or came up with something creative, I automatically thought, *How can I make this bigger?* My mind looked for a way to make it ten times better. Pushed by that thinking, sometimes my idea grew by four or eight times rather than the ten I'd planned for. Still, the growth was never disappointing because it was always bigger and better than when the adventure began.

Each of us is born with an instinctive curiosity. Babies just naturally love to learn. Few consider the fact that the basis of their hunger for knowledge comes from looking into the future. Think about all the times you answered a toddler who asked *what if* and *why*.

When the little guy pulls the laundry basket down on top of him, his curiosity has gotten the best of him. The wheels in his tiny brain begin to turn when he sees a stray piece of cloth. *What will happen if I pull that?* When the whole thing comes crashing down, he learns something about future planning.

A burnt finger starts with the question *What if I touch that iron?* And the reward of a cookie teaches him that saying please can instigate a pleasant ending. With every curious adventure, little ones build a mental database of future potential.

I never outgrew that state of natural curiosity, and I can't decide if my stubbornness drives my curiosity, or they interact the other way around. I'm pretty sure the two create another sort of flywheel—curiosity breeds stubbornness and stubbornness triggers my curiosity. When I enter a room, I consider the layout and ask why. *Why does a waitress have four tables in those areas of the restaurant? Why did the engineers who designed the bridge add those supports? Why did they put the door in that way?* I don't question their abilities or ideas, I'm genuinely inquisitive. And my stubbornness won't accept just any answer. I need a verifiable reason that makes sense. Without that piece of information, my curiosity turns into problem solving, and my mind begins to investigate ways to make the future of the dilemma better—way better.

Start with the Future

Every zero I ever added for myself or other entrepreneurs started by looking into the future. I didn't even realize future thinking was part of my process during my first few ventures; however, two simple questions, *why* and *what if,* have been pressing me to think bigger and find solutions that create massive value for as long as I can remember.

This hit warp speed when I began to engage with Strategic Coach®. Dan Sullivan is a genius with a Unique Ability® to reshape the way you think about your thinking.[5] While my brain naturally works in line with Dan's training, he has given me a toolset to multiply my Unique Ability® and add a zero for everyone I work with.

As I started considering ways to create value for others and perhaps make a few dollars in the process, I discovered my first collaborative business. My father greatly enjoys riding horses. This allowed me to begin riding even before I could walk. And by the time I was six or eight, I accompanied my dad to at least three horse auctions every week. We traveled up to ninety-minutes after school to get to the sale barns. It didn't take long for me to see an opportunity.

> THE ONLY WAY TO MAKE YOUR PRESENT BETTER IS BY MAKING YOUR FUTURE BIGGER.
>
> DAN SULLIVAN

Natural curiosity caused me to consider why some horses brought a higher price than others. As soon as I understood that watching a young rider easily handle a horse, rather than what they assumed was a more experienced adult, impressed potential buyers, I started offering my services to the owners and other horse traders. A horse that doesn't need broken and listens to an inexperienced rider invites more bids. After I discovered I could make a little money riding one horse, I looked for and found my first way to add a zero.

Those owners and traders decided my small fee was more than reasonable for the potentially increased revenue. If I'd been more business savvy at the time, I would have asked for a percentage of the sales. But even at ten or twenty dollars a horse, I netted more zeros in very short period than most fifth graders could make in one year.

Over the next few years, I found myself imagining ways to create value and help solve every problem I encountered. When I got older and started to contemplate how my brain worked, I realized my subconscious constantly digs deeper into what my eyes see and ears hear, and I found myself thinking, *Why does this work that way?* and *How can I reconfigure all the facts and resources and create a bigger outcome for someone else and myself?*

Maybe my extensive time with horses helped me look closer at what can be and further honed my skills at a young age. I spent a great deal of time with those silent beasts. Only a horse lover will understand how much they communicate without saying a word. Working with them emphasized the fact that God gave us four inputs and only one output, and it's important to use them proportionately. So, as I cared for the farm's gentle giants, I learned the art of truly listening for the sake of understanding, not simply to reply. Additionally, grooming, riding, and prepping for sales gave me plenty of alone time to ponder all the ways to make the future better.

My dad and I were glued at the hip during those years. Naturally, I ended up being there when he talked to other businesspeople and friends. Looking back, I realize the listening skill the horses taught me gave me a head start on the road to success. Humans instinctively size up the things around them, so as my dad conversed with other businessmen and horsemen, my brain soared into double-time sizing them up. That one had a nice truck; this one had better horses; a third just bought a new horse trailer. And the last guy—even at ten, I wondered, *Why does it seem like he's out to lunch?* I knew I didn't want to be guy number four when I grew up no matter what it took. And watching them made me wonder what made the difference between the first three and the last. Like the horses, I didn't speak, but I stayed hyper-vigilant, always pursuing why and maintaining perspective to truly learn and understand. The contrast pushed my curiosity into high gear, and I started asking myself, *How did they earn enough money to buy those nice things?* I didn't know it then, but that passion for discovery was worth way more than time spent in a conventional classroom.

By my early teens, natural curiosity motivated me to learn how to maximize the impact of a mower to reduce the time required to cut a field. I also learned to take those same resources and combine them to provide value to others with my very first company, Chad's General Services (CGS), where I leveraged resources at my fingertips and focused on mowing bank-owned outparcels for future development. It caused me to constantly ask questions and find answers. Like a toddler exploring the world, I soaked in every bit of information presented to me with the understanding it would be helpful in the future.

Molding Perspective

Every day presents opportunities to embrace and change our reality. The ability to shift your perspective begins in the way you think about problems. Two toddlers burn their fingers on hot coals. One learned not to touch the red and white remnants; the other vows never to go near another campfire. So, while the first child enjoys s'mores as a teen, the other misses out on the fun. The only difference is the perspective.

Adults, older siblings, and cousins shape most of those three-year-olds' viewpoints. When parents make excuses for their children, bail them out every time they make a mistake, or constantly overreact to minor mishaps, that response becomes instilled in the children. They begin to view curiosity as a painful thing instead of a method to move ahead in life. On the other hand, dads and moms who blow off boo-boos and refuse to pass along their own fears and insecurities can produce offspring whose natural curiosity grows beyond that of their peers.

Even without parental coaching, some people's natural curiosity succumbs to the tyrant of fear. But that fear mind-set can be reset. It takes work and begins by looking and listening. Problems abound, and each of us has the gifts and abilities to take care of more than we think. Adding a zero begins by always looking for solutions and maintaining an "I can already do that" attitude.

When I started riding those horses at the sale barns, I couldn't buy a horse. I didn't even have a pony to sell. But a collaboration mindset opened the door to endless possibilities. I suppose it helped that eight-year-olds seldom focus on what can't be done. In my case, the opportunity looked as obvious as a billboard with blinking lights planted in my front yard, and the solution seemed simple. I had no idea curiosity drove me or that true collaborative value creation was my passion.

Today, I use this principle on a little larger scale. Rather than looking for ways to change the outcome of an afternoon or using my natural curiosity to learn random skills that may or may not be useful in the future, I picture and plan for the realities that exist for entrepreneurs and industries all over the world. And not simply for today, but five, ten, fifteen, or twenty years down the road. And perhaps one of my greatest assets is the curiosity of the eight-year-old that still lives deep inside.

When I work with others to help them discover ways to change their mindset and begin to leverage the Just Add a Zero value-creation methods themselves, I encourage them to start with a blank sheet of paper and list things they know to be facts about their business, team, situation, opportunities, and even their obstacles. Dan Sullivan presents The R-Factor Question®, "If we were having this discussion three years from today, and you were looking back over those three years, what has to have happened in your life, both personally and professionally, for you to feel happy with your progress?" I love to begin with that scenario. This question is brilliant and so impactful to get what's deep inside to come to the surface.

I invite entrepreneurs I meet with for the first time to choose a specific future date, and then I walk them to the date exposing ways to add zero's along the way.

I ask questions regarding the future of their personal life, and we extrapolate the things that are important to them. We write down targets, the things that will get them there.

- What will your professional life look like?

- Where will your children be?

- What does your bank account look like?

Some people need to set specific dates before they decide the *what*, others assign dates to the list after they've written it all down. Either way, the list needs a timeline to help your brain see each item as truly achievable. And the beautiful thing about this process is that even if we don't meet the goal, we're still further ahead than if we hadn't tried.

Achieving the goal isn't nearly as important as believing the goal is achievable. Without that change in mindset, we can't focus on the steps we need to take to reach the next milestone. Your mindset is paramount.

Looking at the future as a realm of possibility begins to shift the mindset and opens the doors of curiosity. In order to move into the future on that piece of paper, we ask, "What if?"

- What if I started my own supply business and leveraged a collaboration partner who already has resources and the same routes to deliver to serve my need and my competitors for less?

- What if I created an app that connected buyers and sellers in my industry and sold my current business?

- What if I started a school to train aspiring individuals to enter my industry to resolve the staffing shortage?

The what ifs go on and on, and with each one, our brains have to change focus until finally we're forced to restate the facts. This enables you to see the real potential of embracing your current friction to unlock all you ever wanted. I call this Identifying the Connection of seemingly Abstract Adjacent Lateral Patterns or iCAALP. By envisioning these facts and patterns as moving laterally and letting curiosity see ways for them intersect, you will often find them way more valuable than their separated state. This collaboration is at the heart of the Just Add A Zero thinking.

Leverage What's Between the Facts

Most people think facts are a definitive obstacle in our futuristic adventure. And while this concept isn't entirely wrong, the true deterrent is the way we look at those facts, and more importantly, the connection between those facts. Remember

> YOU CANNOT SOLVE THE PROBLEM WITH THE SAME MIND THAT CREATED IT.
> ALBERT EINSTEIN

the examples above that outlined two perspectives that produced two completely different outcomes. What if you could train your brain to see both the future and the present as you can the past? Considering both to create the best outcome possible is the essence of JAAZ.

If we consider our list of what might happen in the future, it's easy to start naming all the reasons why it will never work. I'm not a poker player; however, I know how people look at cards. As soon as the hands are dealt, each player starts his assessment. One person thinks, *This is a lousy hand.* The guy across the table has the same variety of suits and numbers. The fact is both players have bad hands; however, the second player restates the facts: *This is a horrible hand. But if everyone has a hand this bad, my odds increase. Plus, if I can keep my composure, I might be able to convince the rest of them I'm sitting good cards long enough to get a better card in the next flop.* Champion players don't accept the facts at face value; they restate them as opportunities.

Most of us have experienced lunches in which the coffee was the highlight of the meeting. Complaints that follow these seemingly useless encounters abound; however, even the most distasteful meeting has potential when you restate the facts. Granted, you may decline the next sixteen invitations from that guy. But if you take the details of the meeting and peel back the onion, or recast the facts, you may find an opportunity to change your life.

Meeting with less successful and unengaging businesspeople can quickly show you voids in their industries. Many of these kinds of leaders can't see the forest for the trees because they're doing things the way they've always been done, yielding only the standard, or less than standard, outcomes that have always been. These are ripe for JAAZ. By restating the facts and pursuing the connections that exist between the facts, you can create exponential value. It's even possible to develop a recurring business model to fill the hole. This less than inspirational leader then becomes your first collaboration partner, and others in his industry will appreciate your innovation. When we take the "what's required mindset" and transform it into an opportunistic mindset, we add zeros with every FILM removal and leveraging of existing markets.

All over the world, fear paralyzes—fear of the unknown, fear of letting someone down, and fear of failure or looking foolish. The entire world shifts ninety degrees when we adjust our perspective and restate our facts. "That will never happen" changes to "What will it take to make it happen?" Fear of losing a paycheck turns into finding creative and beneficial ways to save and budget for the company that at the same time allows us to forge ahead.

Looking at the true facts enables us to understand the exact variables without the emotion. Then we can use logic and association to determine the best way each could connect to create a bigger future for everyone involved. Restating the facts is the first step in transforming perspective. In its earliest stages, you will begin to see yourself diverging from the status quo. Everyone else is gathering in the pool of conventional thinking. You, on the other hand, as you continue to apply this mindset, will stand alone. It may seem like a lonely place until you begin to reap the benefits. Then others will want to follow you.

Restating the facts creates thought leaders with bigger margins. While everyone else operates conventionally, the person who gives the facts a

> IF YOU DON'T LIKE THE RULES, CHANGE THE GAME.

positive spin moves into an entirely new dimension gobbling up their market share. Though everyone starts on the same playing field, with the same friction and the same facts, someone who doesn't allow the facts to be excuses becomes the person who delivers more value with better margins. People who embrace the facts and use them to their advantage mint a new system. They can use this system to not only increase volume, but also name their price because they have the only solution—all based on what looked like hopeless facts. I am often heard saying that looking backwards, every time I did not like the rules, I changed the game.

Friction Identification

One of the biggest differences between people who add zeros and those who become complacent with the existing conditions is the way they deal with friction.

Friction is unavoidable. It exists everywhere, and like the film on your electronics, some choose to ignore it or work around it. Others who haven't learned its value put friction in a negative light; however, friction has been the mother of some of the most tremendous value creation inventions. Smelly human waste inspired outhouses, then flush toilets, and ultimately a huge opportunity for one of my companies—we placed RFID tracking systems on large waste containers in 211 cities across the US to track and shape the behavior of individuals' recycling. The tedious time it took to travel created wheels, then engines, then airplanes. But none of it would have happened if someone hadn't asked the questions. What if we harnessed the wind? Why can't we use steam as a propellent? How would it affect the quality of life if water were more readily available?

I see friction as potential because every obstacle creates opportunity. Elon Musk saw friction in the space industry.

Spaceships are expensive. He asked the questions. Why do they cost so much? What can we do to make them more affordable? How will this benefit all of humankind? And the first privately owned liquid-fueled re-usable rocket was born.

However, most people tend to begin their friction identification in a different vein than Musk building a rocket. People discontented with their current position often don't understand that looking at the simplest things makes all the difference. They think a move to a new field or company will provide peace. But before we make drastic changes, we should start by looking for friction right where we are. For example, a businessman working in loss mitigation at the bank feels trapped. He wants out; however, rather than make a big move, I would encourage him to start to look for friction in his department. Because he's on the inside, he will be able to identify the problems better than anyone else. Plus, if he finds friction in his department, it will likely be applicable to other departments and other banks he connects with in his daily work. Now, he has relief in his job as well as the potential for his own company. And if he chooses to become entrepreneurial, he already has a relationship with his first prospective client—his current boss!

Boredom and stagnation cause folks to feel like they want to make career moves. However, before you pull up stakes, I recommend you look for problems (of course, I call them opportunities) and leverage the tools you find in this book to identify solutions. Friction identification means opportunity identification. If you can start where you are and identify friction, you may discover you'll create enough adventure to make the job more interesting, and most likely get a promotion, or at minimum, a raise. On the other hand, you might end up starting your own consultation company with clients built in. But you will miss both if you don't start where you are. Obviously, you can move to another company and hit the reset button, but often you simply add risk and forgo the real opportunity and investments you have already made. Practice JAAZ first, you will not be sorry.

Unfortunately, too many people don't get inquisitive. One person works in the manufacturing industry for twenty years and he feels like he is dying a slow, painful death. He has no idea how to escape. Another person feels stuck. She focused on her kids and job for so long, she lost her identity. Neither tries to see the friction, let alone look for ways to overcome it.

Those who keep sinking in the mire of the friction could be more like Allyson Downey or Kyla Dahrling. They prove that friction identification becomes the catalyst for inventions, solutions, and eliminating competition.

Allyson Downey worked as a Wall Street Banker until her first child was on the way. When the company sidelined her, she created a successful line of baby gear and uses her personal network to create mutually beneficial collaborations.

Kyla Dahrling had to choose between her career and her children when the pharmaceutical company she worked for wouldn't allow her to work part-time. She chose her children and started a business called *Tiny Trucker Company*. One of her company's goals is to provide part-time employment for parents who want to focus on raising a family.[5]

Rather than run from or ignore the friction, people who experience adding zeros keep an eye out for it. It's most often at the center of their innovations and a core driver behind their continued success. In every conversation I have with business leaders, I look for the friction in their industry or their company. And, the good thing is, you don't have to pry. Most folks like to share their friction as complaints, creating a treasure trove for me and those who have a Remove the Film and Just Add a Zero mindset. If we chat long enough, problems will surface as opportunities to remove the film. Then I apply JAAZ to enable me to find solutions.

As you can likely already see, friction identification offers job security and client retention because the solution for friction and growth will naturally create more friction, giving you more opportunities to add exponential value. Embracing the friction and understanding how it works turns each innovation into a never-ending adventure full of opportunity and value creation.

Always Pursue the Why

I spent my first thirty-five years believing the secret to getting ahead was being smarter, working harder, starting earlier, and laboring longer. Some would call it a farming mentality. You won't find many young people with as good a work ethic as the teen who spent summers in the hay field. But as you may have gathered by now, something inside of me asked, *Why? What's the purpose in working harder? What does my future look like if I labor less and focus on creating more value?*

Don't get me wrong, I believe in hard work and gaining knowledge; however, I'm also naturally driven to find ways to create more value with less effort. I don't just want to labor longer; I want a much larger return for the energy I expend. That's why I wouldn't trade natural curiosity for anything in the world.

At some point, it dawned on me that billions of people live and have lived on this planet, and that most likely means that whatever I'm doing someone else has probably already done or at least tried before. Plus, there's a good chance they wrote down some of what they learned. Natural curiosity asked, "What if I could read about someone else's mistakes and avoid them? Then I could just make new mistakes."

So, I began reading everything I could get my hands on. Today, I read about two books a week, listen to countless podcasts, and spend plenty of time learning on YouTube and GPT, or as I like to call it, "modern-day college," to expand my knowledge at a rate never before attainable. Natural curiosity allows me to consume a lot of data, and my wiring enables me to run it through a myriad of options to discover the best way to leverage what I have learned to create value not seen before. By examining what's been done before and exploring what can be, I can apply it to whatever I find myself involved in now or in the future. The knowledge my curious nature soaks up creates a database of information that puts me at a tremendous advantage.

For instance, in one of my earlier businesses, I was fortunate to be able to witness firsthand over one thousand businesses' value and operational differences. Looking back, this time period gave me a crash course that equated to a masters education when combined with my natural curiosity and pursue why mindset.

I constantly asked myself questions. For instance, why did one landscaper who served the same clients do so much better than another landscaper? And what drives the consistent growth of this residential service company. Anyone can provide such service, but these guys are getting it right!

> WANT TO CHANGE YOUR LIFE? CHANGE THE QUESTIONS YOU ARE ASKING.
> JIM KWIK

One national home builder applied Just Add a Zero thinking to facilitate outfitting new hires with all their communications needs in a unique fashion during the first day's onboarding. After many renditions of Removing the FILM, we integrated a comprehensive solution that included one of my firms handling their needs across the entire southeast. This value proposition combined the best of our two organizations for a true win-win. The first ninety days effectiveness numbers for new team members increased by 50 percent, and team satisfaction increased 100 percent.

The national home builder wanted to create a competitive advantage as they increased sales and expanded their market. My team dug deeper by pursuing the why. We uncovered the impact of having the new associates outfitted, trained, and ready on day one. By making this a priority, the company set a welcoming tone for each new hire. Additionally, they sent the message that the organization expected them to begin creating value the first day by providing the right tool set. My organization customized their training, provided contact inclusion, and gave them all the components to empower each new associate to hit the ground running. This program grew our recurring revenue by 40 percent while facilitating a smooth initial first impression with our collaborator's new associate. After a number of years, I am happy to report that many of those associates now run their own organizations in the industry, and I am fortunate to still be doing business with many of them. Pursuing the why with natural or intentional curiosity to look beyond the immediate request can have life changing impacts to both parties.

By leading with the mindset of Removing the FILM, I have a constant focus that results in making it easy to do business with my companies. When I started one of my technology-based businesses, I encountered those two landscapers I mentioned above. I personally visited both on a regular basis, but I made sure I arrived at the more successful landscaper's office before 6:30 a.m. because that's the time his crews left every morning. The second landscaper's trucks pulled out about 7:15 a.m., and some didn't leave the lot until 7:30 a.m. I immediately realized these guys were going to hit traffic. By analyzing the time they would spend sitting in traffic and estimating their average salary, the number of guys in the truck, and the production impact, I surmised this customer's later start cost him approximately $1.7 million each year. He counted on me to manage his team's communication tools, not his margin or production; however, my natural curiosity helped him increase his profit, and it made him want to do more business with me.

During my first year in the mobile technology business, I never traveled outside the belt loop of Charlotte, North Carolina, still, I put nearly one hundred thousand miles on my vehicle distributing mobile communication devices. And with each visit, natural curiosity set in consuming the good, the bad, and the ugly for my customers. *Why does this company excel? Why is this national homebuilder expanding and this other one losing people? Why is this company affected by the market? Why does this business thrive during a recession?*

In the spirit of Just Add A Zero, during the second year, I put over twenty vehicles on the road with routes like ice cream trucks—one for each production neighborhood—servicing each builder, landscaper, roofer, plumber, etc.

Casting the Vision

Asking why allows us to dig deeper and understand the facts at a root level, which empowers us to look into the future to see the real possibilities others would say are invisible to the masses. It's not easy for everyone. Many times, it's as simple as seeing how two things connect—facts about a business, people in the industry, and even ideas that look as though they have no overlap. I recently talked to a bookkeeping franchisor outside of San Diego about this strategy. He heard me say just add a zero, but the methodology seemed abstract to him. He didn't see how his business could possibly use this philosophy.

I encouraged him to write down two or three things that he would like to see happen that seem completely disconnected. Then I challenged him to think about what it would look like if those two things came together. What would be the outcome? When we do that, even the mind that doesn't naturally see a means to connect them will begin to find ways to make them work together. I also encouraged him to think bigger to envision those connections with the much larger magnitude of outcomes that present themselves when connecting seemingly abstract facts and resources. And with that realization, envisioning a new future begins—a future with possibilities of adding zeros.

When I read *Driven* by Douglas Brackmann, PHD and Randy Kelley, MBA, I had major revelations about myself. From the first page, I felt as though the author described me as if he'd met me. He talks about Navy Seals, extreme athletes, and entrepreneurs and how we are wired a bit differently than the rest of the world. I have what he calls a hunter brain, a person who wakes up every morning chasing the lion.[6]

My occipital lobe seems to work overtime. That's the back section of your brain, and though it's the smallest part, we need it to process visual signals the retina sends. It processes shapes, textures, colors, and distance. Additionally, it's the place that remembers faces and what the room looks like. Everyone, even a blind person, counts on the occipital lobe to maneuver through life. For those who are sight impaired, the occipital lobe creates pictures based on sounds and touch. It helps the blind as well as the sighted navigate in the dark by creating images for us even when we can't see.

Studies show that as much as humans would like to believe they can multitask, it's impossible. On the other hand, you can multi-think. As my eyes and ears take in information, my occipital lobe visualizes every byte—yes, even what I hear. I think with the back part of my brain; therefore, I have a constant influx of vision. Then my occipital lobe transfers the information to my frontal lobe, the part of the brain with executive function. I begin to contemplate and reason and then associate the new information with things I've learned in the past. Some of this previous information seems useless to the average individual, but I learned long ago that every experience has value. The forward section of my brain runs all these associations and forms thousands upon thousands of connections revealing the abundance of potential that exists in whomever or whatever I'm conversing with or about.

It's not something I can keep from happening. It's just the way my brain is wired. If I'm reading, having a conversation, or listening to a speaker, I'm also searching for friction and thinking about how I can add a zero to those facts. In every engagement, my occipital lobe scans for opportunities to connect the most abstract things. I worry some people might think it's rude that I find snags and shortfalls they weren't even looking for. But as I focus on the person I'm talking to and their business, I can see the innate power within them and their company, as well as the things I can connect to that power and the outcome from them in real time. And as I see the zeros, I must share them.

Add-a-zero thinking helps me ask the right questions when I help others try to expand their endeavors. Nothing peaks a person's curiosity more than when I begin to talk in the exponential. I can see their business and their plans one hundred times bigger, and when I begin to ask the questions that lay the foundation of that added zero mindset, I grab their attention. Envisioning a future with that extra zero fuels my questions and allows me to help them build the framework to solve their dilemma and see increase faster than they imagined.

How Anyone Can Pursue the Why

While curiosity comes naturally to me, anyone with a drive to add zeros can develop it. I've turned this methodology into a course available at SeedSpark.com/growth-ac ademy. SeedSpark Growth Academy was born because I believe so strongly these skills can be learned and should be passed on. Students are not only trained in Removing FILM and the JAAZ methodology, but they are also required to mentor the next friction seeker they find.

Curiosity will grow with every question you ask. Some may use the excuse that they don't have any education. But I embrace the fact I have little conventional higher education. In fact, my college experience is limited to a single semester. Everything I know has come to me through natural curiosity and intentionally listening. Access to information is limitless in today's world; there's more than a good chance the only thing holding you back is mindset and a clear path for execution.

My least favorite parental phrase is "because I said so." You'll hear exasperated moms and dads speak it frequently, but when those few words get thrown around casually, they can stifle natural curiosity. Some children have the ability so deeply ingrained that they continually ask questions. The barrage of inquisitiveness causes outsiders to laugh and parents to pull their hair out. For me, I love it. I challenge my teams and my daughters to always find three more questions and to truly seek to understand before judging or solving.

To pursue the why, it's vital to return to a Columbo level of questioning. The late 1960's detective always had one more question. By the final question, he knew the answer and had solved the mystery, yet he still asked it. You don't even need to speak the questions; it's enough to allow them to tumble around in your brain while you remain vigilant in looking for the answer. But asking the questions and continuing to ask until the most unrelated facts work together is essential.

When you pursue the why and log the answers in your brain, you will spot the differences that will enable you to be better today than you were yesterday. Those questions will empower you to find the friction and uncover possible connections resulting in bigger outcomes.

Go back to that blank piece of paper I mentioned earlier in the chapter. Create your list of things you want to do or have. Then add dates to your list. When would you like those things to happen? Next begin asking the questions. What stands in your way? What if you connected with someone? Who do you know that can help you? Where could you look for help? How did someone else make that happen? Why do you want it? Why should you have it? And the most important question—What's sitting right in front of me that, if I connect it to something else right in front of me, can impact the outcome exponentially and possibly have a domino effect in creating the outcome I want?

Include things on your list that seem completely opposite one another, then sleep on it. Use your brain's natural ability and the power of your subconscious to work while you rest to give you great ideas and answer your deepest questions. And if your brain begins to make excuses or tell you why you can't, restate the facts.

One key to allowing your natural curiosity to kick in is to enter every situation as if you know nothing about what's going on. I'm invited to help add zeros to businesses and individuals' lives each day all over the planet. Even if I have a great deal of awareness regarding the industry or type of company, I begin from the standpoint of not knowing anything. I challenge myself to see everything through a new set of eyes and envision the business ten times bigger than it is now. That view of the future then fuels my question. My future-based questions pique their curiosity and often spurs their own natural curiosity, so they learn to ask the right questions.

People who successfully Pursue Why are lifelong learners. They read or listen to books, articles, podcasts, and more. If you want to train your brain in this skill, find subjects that interest you. Then take notes, learn from other's mistakes, and find a way to let the material transform your thinking.

Even recognizing given information won't work for your situation can be a valuable lesson if you'll accept it.

You'll also want to re-evaluate everything you previously considered useless information or wasted experiences. Every part of your past, even the unpleasant experiences, holds valuable data that has the potential to tie into friction and give you a unique perspective and an equally anomalous solution. A dear friend of mine, Dr. Nik from Toronto, Ontario, helps highly successful entrepreneurs develop a mindset that will allow them to reach beyond high performance. He has taught me a lot about my ability to re-frame past challenges and resources and embrace them from a new perspective. This thinking takes us from a what was done *to* me to a what was done *for* me mindset. His work on facilitating breakthroughs and helping people reach their full potential is astounding.

The key is to use your natural curiosity to spot differences, then logging that information for later use. When you constantly look for new data and always save it for tomorrow, you begin to see every interaction as a future opportunity to create value for others. You'll also begin to develop an attitude that sees every person as someone you can learn from.

Constantly identifying friction and reshaping your mindset into a questioning, fact stating, future thinking mentality will set you on the path to the next step in our process of adding zeros.

CHAPTER 3

Maintain Perspective

If you change the way you look at things, the things you look at change.

—Wayne Dyer

I STARTED MAKING CONNECTIONS in that sale barn before I turned nine, opening the door to meeting horse enthusiasts who needed a trainer for their horse. So, for a monthly fee, I got to do what I love to do—hang out with the horses and train them for other owners. Pretty soon, I started trading, buying, and selling horses, all thanks to my Dad.

During these early years, I learned how to see life from my customer's perspective. I saw their problems and opportunities, and considered how those headaches made them feel. Sometimes I identified the friction in their ideas before they did. Every time I successfully solved one person's problem, I saw a new one and moved forward. This ability to take on my customer's perspective eliminated my competition—not because I put them out of business. I had no competition because no one looked at things the way I did. My mind doesn't begin with a product or service to sell. Instead, I view everything from a value creation perspective. And if perchance someone else had already developed this mindset, there's a good chance we would start working together and serving each other.

The first big payoff for one of those connections came just after I turned eighteen.

During high school, I participated in team roping all over the US and did pretty well. By the time I graduated, I had won the finals four years in a row as well as many regional and even a few nationals. In the summer of my eighteenth year, I traveled to the United States Team Roping Championship in Guthrie, Oklahoma. We were competing at the Lazy E, one of the most famous indoor rodeo arenas in the United States, when my dad called early one morning.

"Hey Chad, you remember that guy from Fort Mill you sold that pony to a few years back ?"

"The guy who bought it for his twelve-year-old daughter? Yeah, what's he up to?"

"Well, he started this store that sells western clothing and Purina feed, and he is struggling. He's looking to sell it. I thought you and I might want to buy it."

On that day, I just wanted to finish well in the national finals, but when I returned to Charlotte, we met with the man and structured a deal. Before I knew it, I had sold the general services company, started paying six hundred dollars a month to rent a small store building on a very high traffic corner, and Dad and I owned a feed and western shop not far from North Carolina's largest city.

Through the Eyes of the Customer

Too often, profit margins drive a business's inventory and pricing as well as their practices. Let's face it, even a non-profit must make enough money to pay the staff. However, when we fall into the trap of what's in it for me and forget to see what

> THE ONLY THING THAT MATTERS IS HOW OTHER PEOPLE SEE THEIR FUTURE AND HOW YOU CAN HELP THEM WITH THAT FUTURE.
>
> UNKNOWN

the business looks like through the eyes of the customer, we set ourselves up for failure. Always remember: the only thing that matters is how other people see their future and how you can help them with that future.

I knew for my new endeavor to succeed, I needed to put myself in my patrons' shoes. What do they perceive as complications? Problems can seem insurmountable. I prefer to look at them as friction, because friction has a solution—a little lubricant, a bit of effort, and the friction can be conquered, at least until the next wave of friction hits.

First, I recognized that people who buy feed and western wear need things like cattle gates and panels. Plus, those horse guys all have livestock trailers, utility trailers, and dump trailers. That means they all need hitches and wiring to accommodate the brakes on their trucks. So, to reduce their friction, and thanks to a dear friend who has passed, I learned how to install heavy duty hitches and wiring. Ed Jamieson was the CEO of a chemical company. And though he didn't need the money, he collaborated with me and taught me how to install gooseneck trailer hitches and brake controllers. He had the equipment and the knowledge, and I had the determination and the customers. After working all day, he and I would be in his garage until nine or ten o'clock taking care of vehicles so they could pull those brand-new trailers.

The property I rented sat on a busy corner just a half hour from Charlotte, and we'd attracted enough business that folks looked our way when they passed by. So, when a lady I knew needed to sell a trailer, she called. "Chad, I buy all my feed from you, and I notice there's a lot of traffic that passes by your place. I have this trailer I don't need anymore. Do you think it would be too much trouble to sell it for me?"

I stopped by her house the next morning, picked up the horse trailer, and pulled it onto the store lot. It was a beautiful, sunny day, and by evening, I'd sold it for the amount she wanted plus a few hundred dollars to keep for myself. It seemed like adding horse trailers to the inventory made sense.

I'd only attended college for a few months, and the subject of how car dealers and other big ticket inventory places could afford their merchandise never came up. But I was determined to figure out how to get horse trailers on my lot. Within a year, my store had a million and a half dollars' worth of floor-plan or front-end inventory. In other words, I connected with horse trailer manufacturers and distributors who collaborated with large banks to facilitate floor-plan inventory. In short, I put a small down payment on each trailer, had them sit on my lot interest free for a period, then either sold them or paid interest on them until they sold. Hello, inventory management.

Natural curiosity and maintaining the perspective of my clients pushed me to explore ways to help horsemen who needed bigger trailers and better equipment for their farms. I realized that farmers, especially horse guys, need financing to move to the next level in their field. Horses are a huge expense, and only a handful win those large purses at the rodeos and horse shows. So, I connected with banks that would allow me to offer financing to horsemen ready to purchase my new inventory, and then I added a leasing option. From their perspective, a trip to the bank takes up valuable time. By solving their problem, I added a zero in my column. I also got my first taste of recurring revenue. This has proven to pay me so many dividends. I took this knowledge and started a leasing company to support my GPS tracking business later.

While we generally start our search for friction within our own company, there is tremendous value in looking at those you serve. When we take a closer look at why those we serve are thinking about terminating our contract or changing services, we might discover the biggest problem is we aren't listening. When we lose our customers' perspectives, we will lose their trust and their business.

Connecting the Future to the Past

Adding zeros begins by envisioning the future, but it builds on what we know from the past. Maintaining perspective means remembering how we got where to where we are today. Those lessons I learned in my twenties never lose significance.

> YOU CAN'T CONNECT THE DOTS LOOKING FORWARD YOU CAN ONLY CONNECT THEM LOOKING BACKWARDS.
>
> STEVE JOBS

When I look backwards, I see horses, horse trailers, feed, tack, Nextel, IT, software, data center, leasing, investment firm, GPS, real estate, self-storage, general construction, and more. My job is connecting the dots to find the common thread in those disconnected areas. What's been the one common thread throughout the years? In my case, it's been my *better is infinite* mindset and desire to create and provide value. This means every day and every business has become an opportunity that transcends business models. It's not about the business; it's about the value you create inside the business. Value adds zeros.

Each of those whys we asked as we considered our future were formed in our past. To expand exponentially, we have to look at where we came from. How did I get here? Why have we done it this way? When you take those answers and apply the value component, you change the game. How can I take what I've learned and create even more value?

The past has the potential to teach us amazing things. Our mistakes, and the mistakes of others, if we let them, help us make adjustments that will improve the value we provide. And remembering what has worked gives us a foundation to build on. Danger sets in when we let past success convince us we don't need to do anything as we move into the future. The film of complacency and elevating the status quo kill even the most profitable businesses and stall promising careers.

On the other hand, if we allow the perspective of our past to be the catalyst for our natural curiosity, the possibilities are endless.

For instance, I hear many people describe past experiences as wastes of time. Have you considered the difference the experience can make if you look at it from a different perspective? I never allow myself to view even the most negative experiences as a waste. Would I ever do that again? Probably not. I've already done it. Nevertheless, when I put my natural curiosity to work on that tiny piece of my past marvelous things transpire. Either I find a valuable lesson, develop a cool new system, or I learn what not to do in the future. The only difference between me and the person who has wasted his time is our perspective.

Changing our Perspective

When we examine the obstacles, we often find more emotions than actual problems. How a person makes us feel turns into an excuse for a poor reaction

> HE WHO ASKS QUESTIONS, CANNOT AVOID THE ANSWERS.
> CAMEROON PROVERB

or inaction. Anxiety, stress, even love for our family and friends can appear to stand in the way of our list of future endeavors. And sometimes the roadblocks are real.

"I don't have the finances to make that happen."

"That other person stands between me and that position."

"A pandemic shut down the world."

Embrace the interference. Even in the case of emotional disturbance, in order to move ahead, we have to own the obstacle and then figure out how to get around it. We literally change the problem.

We all have emotions. Humans are driven by wants, needs, fear, and greed, but when we separate the facts from those elements, we can isolate the exact variables and then logically explore the best way to apply those variables to our situation or begin to see how the facts play together. Immediately, a new mindset begins to develop. It may take a while for a total transformation; however, by simply restating the data, you'll see a divergence from the status quo.

Constantly returning to that principle of restating the facts for their authentic expression will go a long way in helping maintain the proper perspective. For instance, we live in a world where everything is done to us.

"He ran into me."

"She made me drop everything."

"My manager fired me."

One word transforms the mindset. Instead of living in the realm of what was done *to* me, those who add zeros exist in a world of what was done *for* me.

"He ran into me" becomes "I am glad we bumped into each other. Otherwise, I would have never found my next collaboration partner."

"She made me drop everything" turns into "I would have never seen those numbers combine that way to create this whole new product."

"My manager fired me" morphs to "Without my last manager letting me go, I'd never have started this company."

With this new perspective, we see ourselves move ahead, and as we continue to apply this new pattern, we enjoy an entirely new outlook.

Building on Friction

Maintaining perspective allows you to build on the friction you identified as you pursued the why. Intentionally seeing the opportunity from each party's perspective—both immediate and long term and, most specifically, how it affects each business—empowers you to communicate at a higher level and build trust. Plus, when you ask yourself, "How does the customer or client feel and how does this change their perspective?" you begin to be able to provide value above and beyond your competition. In fact, as I said in the beginning of this chapter, they aren't really competition anymore. You have changed the game and allowed yourself to write your own rules. Refreshing and rewarding for you, your team, and your customers or clients—not to mention considerably more profitable.

Each team member has the potential to build on friction identification and leverage their own market to create value. Whatever causes you the most deep-seated pain will reveal the friction that needs your attention. And after identifying that friction worthy of your attention, you may ask yourself a couple questions. Does this affect only me, my department, or my company? Or does this also affect others—those in the same department, the same size company, or same industry? As you begin to get yes after yes, your excitement should be building. You may have just found the path to your next You. With every affirmative, value builds and your depth of market deepens, allowing you to create value for even more businesses and individuals. By finding the solution to the most frustrating part of your job with JAAZ thinking, you can turn your team, your company, every similar company in your city or state—possibly the entire industry—into clients.

In order to become this type of person, you have to shift your perspective to one that goes beyond a mere employee to someone who recognizes and solves friction. Those who maintain a why-based perspective constantly ask, "How does this affect, feel and impact everyone involved?" This level of value creation requires you to consider all perspectives.

The same thing happens when that employee searches for friction in clients' companies. I get excited when a team member comes to me with this type of RTF (Remove the FILM) opportunity. Helping create new entrepreneurs is one of my greatest pleasures.

Becoming hyper-aware of everything that's going on around you allows you to identify the friction and embrace it to create value others can't or don't want to see. You can grow to the point of forecasting the friction. (Sidenote: If you get this good at seeing friction and quantifying the market, you may have to slow it down. This can raise a lot of eyebrows in conventional boardrooms.) The solution to the friction will always cause more friction. By keeping an eye out for it, you can get ahead of it and turn into the person that people want to follow. Regardless of your role, if you continually search for answers, you can eventually name your price and become an industry leader or creator. And who knows, you might even go global or, as in Elon Musk's case, to space.

In addition to maintaining perspective in the realm of friction, I encourage our staff to go beyond just seeing what our clients see. I want them to consider how our actions make clients and vendors feel, and then dig deeper to find out why they feel that way. Does it have something to do with their past? Did something I said accidentally hit a nerve? Looking beyond the bare facts builds empathy and relationship. It makes people want to keep working with you long after the current business transaction. I often say out loud, until robots do business with robots, you are much better off studying the human side of business.

Keeping my clients' perspective in view provided me the opportunity to build exponentially on friction from the beginning. While building the Nextel phones distributor business, I continued to look for friction beyond my own business. I noticed that one problem I faced was applicable to many businesses. Everyone's mobile bills were all over the board. I began tracking the cost per user per month and discovered that the bills inconsistent and incorrect. That's when I applied RTF and JAAZ. I created a new service and, ultimately, a new business audited mobile invoices each month.

Very soon, I had to apply RTF and employ JAAZ again when this new company scaled to the point it created a new kind of friction. I needed to build a team to serve my growing client list, and the conventional hire, train, repeat method couldn't keep up with the demand. This friction and my entree into the IT business had opened my eyes to the capabilities of custom software. Applying RTF sent me searching for a few *Whos* to help me create an application to assist in auditing the wireless bills and keeping up with the demand this Just Add a Zero business created.

After a couple of interviews and some long nights writing the business logic to save millions on those cellular bills, I found my Whos. Though, instead of hiring them to create only this software, I decided to create a software business—another Just Add A Zero result.

The thinking that drove me to find a solution for the friction was frighteningly similar to many of my clients in the wireless business. BlackBerry® was gaining popularity, and I had recently signed a deal with SPRINT® and Blackberry to create the first Blackberry® Store in the world. (Yes, I'm aware how that ages me.) This ability to create apps gave me an insight to friction in other businesses I served, and more importantly, it opened the door for a new way to create value for those who already trusted one or more of my organizations. Delivering these apps via the Blackberry increased collaboration between my two organizations as they were focused on being a hero to the same clients creating growth for everyone.

The secret to building on friction is consistency. You solve the first friction, maximize it, then solve the new friction. Some friction will be small. Other friction will become the catalyst to huge impact for you and your businesses.

The friction I created by solving that initial friction actually opened the door to an entirely new business—this continues to happen over and over. By watching for friction in the lives of my clients and maintaining their perspectives, I've been able to build many successful organizations and created growth for hundreds more.

How Anyone Can Maintain Perspective

The list you created in the last chapter allowed you to begin to see the possibilities of the future. As you contemplate the vision, the list will probably grow. Seeing the potential emboldens us to imagine even more—to conceptualize those zeros.

For example, maintaining perspective can transform job interviews. When you visit a prospective employer or even a prospective client with a mindset of adding zeros, you automatically look for ways to create value for the person in the chair across from you, sometimes in ways that have nothing to do with the job opening. If the interviewer doesn't appreciate your forward thinking, you probably don't want to work for or with that company. Either that or you just may be running a similar company within a few short years.

JUST ADD A ZERO   65

In the same way, it's important for the person doing the hiring to keep a future thinking perspective. Rather than look for the person who is right for the position today, we need to ask the question, will he or she benefit the company ten years from now? Does this person have the drive and the core values that will enhance the atmosphere of your business for years to come? If you can't see them working for your expanded vision, then you shouldn't hire them now. On the other hand, if those same people don't fit today but can add zeros in three years, you may consider finding a way to pay them whatever they're worth. Looking backwards, those people have been some of my most solid investments.

The primary goal of maintaining perspective is continually looking at the world through the eyes of the person you want to create value for. This is the embodiment of walking a mile in someone else's shoes. To be truly successful in the Just Add a Zero philosophy, you have to step back from what's best for you and search for the thing that will create the greatest value for everyone.

Maintaining the perspective of others is what makes JAAZ and Friction Identification to Leverage the Market counter cultural. In a world where the majority live with a me-first mentality, you will quickly set yourself apart when prospective clients see that you care about their needs at least as much as your own and oftentimes more.

Those looking out for themselves might net a nice one-time payout, but those who maintain perspective will build trust and repeat business that will add zeros for years to come.

CHAPTER 4

Take Ownership

*Something happens when you feel ownership.
You no longer act like a spectator or consumer,
because you're an owner.*

—Bob Goff

B Y THE TIME I got my driver's license, I had already added more zeros to my income than most other teenagers. I had moved from riding horses in sale barns to boarding, training, trading, buying, and selling them. So, when the local banks began buying random lots throughout the Charlotte area, I started connecting the dots. Weeds accumulating on those plots would force them to hire someone to keep them in the good graces of the city. The lots didn't need an immaculate manicure. They would be construction sites within a year or two; however, to keep the rodent and snake population at bay, the tall grass needed knocked down a few times each month.

Living on a farm meant I had a tractor and bush hog, as well as a truck and trailer at my disposal. The bank agreed to pay me fifty dollars an hour to use my equipment to clear those lots. And CTJ General Services was born. By the time I got the call from my dad that led to the purchase of the western store, I had a small team of guys from school working for me to keep up with the demand.

After we've identified our vision and connections, it's time to assess our capabilities and resources. The fifteen-year-old Chad recognized his ability to run a tractor and bush hog as well as his access to equipment that would enable him to use it for others. He took ownership of his small enterprise, created value for the bank and others, and began adding zeros to his wallet.

Identify Your Capability

Earlier, I called everyone a genius. Maybe you laughed at the idea, but I'm not the first person to present this theory. In the late 1900s, Howard Gardner, a Harvard psychologist, disputed the widely held belief that intelligence had but one standard of measure-namely, test taking.[8] He argued intelligence came in nine distinct types, and I would contend there could potentially be even more areas of genius.

Gardner identified these areas of intelligence:

Visual/Spatial—These individuals have the ability to look at a blueprint and see the room. Like me, their occipital lobe runs in overdrive, and they naturally see what can be.

Linguistic/Verbal – This person works best with words and considers the practice of using pictures to create instruction booklets the equivalent of returning to hieroglyphics.

Mathematical—You might think this kind of intelligence belongs to bookkeepers and people who are good with numbers, but people with Mathematical Intelligence see logic, steps, and progressions and apply them in every situation.

Kinesthetic/Bodily—Mechanics, electricians, body builders, and football players have high kinesthetic intelligence. These individuals work well with their hands, and unlike the person with verbal intelligence, they don't mind those pictures in the instruction booklets.

Musical—This one is a bit more obvious. Your friend who can pick up any instrument and make it sound beautiful or always picks the harmony parts when they sing with the radio probably has musical intelligence.

Interpersonal—Some people naturally work well with others. This intelligence type sees the other person's point of view without thinking about it. They make negotiations better than most and have great empathy. The best sales-people have this type of intelligence.

Intrapersonal—Though the word sounds a lot like the last one, and someone with interpersonal intelligence can excel at intrapersonal too, it's the exact opposite. The person with intrapersonal intelligence knows themselves inside and out. They understand their skillset and can sort out their feelings without much assistance.

Naturalistic—Botanists, farmers, park rangers, zoologists, veterinarians, and more understand natural things and can read nature better than others.

Existential—Gardner didn't originally have this on his list, but he eventually decided that those who have "inner wisdom" and are great at contemplating the human condition have a category all their own.

Understanding our Unique Ability and embracing our genius are essential to taking ownership. I believe you can't really know who someone else is until you fully understand who you are. Lee Brower says the world would be a completely different place if we focused on two words—*Take Responsibility.* I have spent an enormous amount of time and effort in doing this myself. Often, asking people to take responsibility projects the notion of someone not doing what they should. I agree this is an important aspect. However, Take Responsibility also means holding yourself accountable and efficiently using the talents and resources you have been blessed with.

Our characteristics and personality traits enhance our Unique Ability and genius. Whether you are an introvert or extravert, and regardless of your leaning toward judging or imaginative, objectivity or feelings, every attribute has the potential to cat-

> EVERYONE IS A GENIUS BUT IF YOU JUDGE A FISH ON ITS ABILITY TO CLIMB A TREE, IT WILL LIVE ITS WHOLE LIFE THINKING IT IS STUPID.
> UNKNOWN

apult you to greatness when you learn how to couple them with your abilities and natural curiosity.

I have personally done a lot of work to uncover the traits that give me my advantage. Unfortunately, it appears to me that less than one percent of the population even attempt to identify the characteristics that make them stand out. They're content to have their DNA, fingerprint, and dental records be their identification markers.

My visionary outlook, analytical thinking, and principled lifestyle are just a few of the qualities that push me to focus on providing value to others. Discovering these unique abilities, characteristics, and traits frees me to share every shortcut and connection as I help others along their own growth journey. I love creating a culture of winning and aspiring to be the best.

Take Inventory of Your Resources

Taking ownership goes further than identifying your abilities, character traits, and personality. It also includes understanding your resources.

Ten-year-old Chad had horses to ride and a dad that liked to go to auctions. Teen Chad had a stable he had helped build as a pre-teen and a corral to couple with his ability to train horses. Pre-adult Chad used a truck, trailer, bush hog, and time to add zeros.

Today my resources include thousands of real connections—I call them geniuses—I've made by implementing my natural curiosity and maintaining perspective to help others.

Obviously, that western shop was one of my first complex organization experiences, and I loved the challenge of growing it into a major farm supply store with my family. Using the resources of relationships, determination, and value creation, I added a Nextel distributorship, and the resources of a car and a staff to run the store let me take those push-to-talk phones to farms and construction sites.

After building the business into a sizeable enterprise, the company itself became a resource. I had sold Purina feeds since I purchased the store. Because our sales were very good, Purina Mills approached me about my feed store becoming the first in their chain of *America's Country Stores*.

Meanwhile, dealing with the Nextel phones had added to my list of resources. First, they forced me to gain an above average understanding of phone plans—plans that changed every thirty days. Second, I identified friction as I watched customers attempt to keep up their constantly changing plans. And finally, I had built a nice list of customers who trusted me.

The phone companies paid me a small amount per phone on a downward sliding scale. But unfortunately, the bills my clients had to read were often wrong and the plans were complex. Since my team had to know the various rate plans anyway, I realized I could use those resources to create ongoing residual income by evaluating my clients' bills and usage each month and recommending the best plan. The big companies were not calling each customer every month to tell them, "We'd like to help you save $200 a month on your phone bill." Industry veterans told me my idea to take a fee to review my client's charges each month would never fly. Natural curiosity, a little Remove the FILM and Just Add a Zero thinking combined with the resources I had in place to sell phones allowed me to connect the dots and create value for my customers. Not only did I save some of my larger customers millions, but my recurring revenue increased by twelve million dollars. I had recurring income, the clients saved tons, and we both added zeros. Think about it. Who would you rather do business with—the company that only provides you with a phone or one who stands behind their suggestion and constantly refines your plan to save you hundreds, thousands, and ultimately millions.

Each resource I leveraged not only added zeros to my income, but it also enabled me to add zeros to my resources and my connections. Those whose primary goal is adding zeros to their bank account have not moved to Major League thinking. They put limits on their dreams.

> IF YOU FIGHT FOR YOUR LIMITATIONS, YOU WILL KEEP THEM
>
> JIM KWIK

Be Creative with Natural Curiosity and Capability

Creativity seems to pour out of musicians and composers. If you pay attention to the many patterns interacting in a symphony or a jazz ensemble, you'll notice that every musician has his own distinct part. Individually, you might not recognize the movement until that instrument picks up the melody line.

I love using my curiosity to discover ways capability, connections, and resources can harmonize in collaboration. Combining them all is my own personal melody line.

When you take ownership, you give yourself permission to write your own part. By using your natural curiosity and capability in innovative ways, you compose something that works in perfect harmony with others.

Ownership means outside the box thinking. It also includes taking credit and responsibility for your ideas. Those who partner with me in business don't downplay their role in the value they bring, and they own it when their suggestions don't work. Ownership understands the difference between failure and gaining information, because even designs that don't go as planned are not failures when they feed our natural curiosity. Friction Identification Leverages the Market every time. It may take more than one attempt, but as Edison is often quoted, "I have not failed. I've just found 10,000 ways that won't work."[9]

My adventure with Nextel began with a bit of creativity. I originally tried to become an official Nextel dealer, but when they came to look at my location, my warehouse style store didn't fit their mold for a retail store. So, Nextel set me up as an agent for a small store outside of Charlotte. I could have met their expectations and let the little counter inside my store do all the work; however, my connect-the-dots mindset knew that the construction guys, electricians, plumbers, brick masons, pavers, and other contractors needed to be at the job sites. Every minute they had to spend driving to take care of administrative needs created friction. So, I broke up the city into what looked like ice cream truck routes, then bought a fleet of Toyota Scions and sent them into all those places subdivisions were being built.

Farmers have the same mentality. Running to town for a phone steals precious time from the fields, but when they saw the time they could save by telling their crews where to take the next load of hay or their wives when they'd be in for dinner, push-to-talk became a farming tool.

Car dealers have some of the biggest employee turnovers of any industry, and each salesman needed a phone. I'd get a call in the evening and head to the car lot the following morning to set up the new guys.

It didn't take long for Nextel to notice the way I leveraged the market. Within a few months, they returned to my unlikely store and offered me a dealership. My sales running through the small store outside of town made it look like that little area had better sales than all of Charlotte. I increased my revenue by getting a dealer's cut as well as recouping the residuals the other dealer had been holding back.

Around that same time, it seemed like a lot of people were making money in real estate. But my natural curiosity asked, "What does that really mean?" I scraped together a few shekels and invested in a commercial building. And even though that piece of real estate didn't do much but create some tax benefits, I kept going. Natural curiosity doesn't stop with one experiment.

I purchased three life insurance policies. The agent showed me the numbers. He brought out the chart and told me if I overfunded them for a few years, I'd have a better return. At just twenty-three, with no debt and no family yet, I didn't really need life insurance. Nevertheless, I discovered I could take loans out against these life insurance policies. Paying back the loans then became the equivalent of paying myself. So, I took out the loans and purchased more commercial buildings I could rent.

The best thing about these random policies was what they taught me about creative or alternative investing. And I began to ask myself, *How can I help these business owners who are making some money but have no idea about alternative investing?* And that inspired me to start an investment firm with investment funds. I now have a vehicle to serve these business leaders who I'm already helping in other areas.

Creativity coupled with curiosity and capability allow me to Just Add a Zero for myself as well as others.

Take Ownership of Your Connections

While I appreciate every person that crosses my path, I've learned that one of the most important parts of taking ownership is being careful about the people I surround myself with. You've probably heard the phrase made famous by motiva-

> YOU ARE THE AVERAGE OF THE FIVE PEOPLE YOU SPEND THE MOST TIME WITH.
>
> JIM ROHN

tional speaker Jim Rohn. "You are the average of the five people you spend the most time with." Yep, those five.

Every close relationship you develop, you will carry with you for the rest of your life. Your childhood buddies still travel with you in some small way. Their presence shaped you. It may have been a small influence, but it made an impact, nevertheless.

Most people never think twice about the kind of people they allow into their lives; however, in the JAAZ philosophy, relationships become paramount. We become very intentional as we select acquaintances and allow them to become friends. People we spend a great deal of time with should bring positivity to our life and spur our natural curiosity.

Consider the path your friend seems to be taking. Let curiosity picture them ten years from now. Do you want to follow them on their journey? Listen to their words. Do they view everything from a can or can't perspective? I repeatedly tell my daughters, "Show me your friends, and I'll show you your future." Can you think of an example where it isn't true in your life?

I took that to heart at a very young age. Despite the fact I'm not really that social—you won't find me hanging out in large crowds—I enjoy interpersonal interactions. Natural curiosity taught me the impact of relationships quite early. Connections at the auctions and watching my dad's interactions helped me understand their importance.

Just as important as intentionally choosing friends is building trust within those relationships. By maintaining perspective and being certain we look at the situation from every angle, especially from the point of view of those most affected by the situation, we create strong ties. People know they can count on us to always act with integrity.

Today, this ideology I developed in the horse stables manifests itself in my business life. First, I would never start a business that doesn't serve and solve the friction in one of these relationships. Second, when I do create an enterprise that can help one of my connections leverage the market, I have built in clients because of the relationships I've built. I maintain a hyper vigilant focus on the ways I can serve.

I recently met with a young man who's new in one of our organizations. He's much smarter than I am, and I let him know that because he's proven himself in our organization, he will soon be meeting people on a global level. I explained that he would need to continue to find ways to create value every day—true value.

Whenever we have an opportunity to meet people who can benefit our future, it's important to look past that benefit as we build the relationship. We need to find their perspective and create real value that will consummate a relationship. Often, we'll get only one chance to create these advantageous connections. But when we look at them through the lens of what we can do for *them* rather than what they can do for *us*, we can add zeros in relationships as well as our future.

If You Can See It

What if you took ownership of every piece of friction you could see? How would it change your day or your perspective? And what if you took that one step further and said, "If I hear about it, I am responsible." The Four Seasons hotel has a policy that

> YOU FAIL ALL THE TIME, BUT YOU AREN'T A FAILURE UNTIL YOU BEGIN TO BLAME SOMEONE ELSE.
>
> BUM PHILLIPS

encourages their team members to take care of their job and one more. For instance, a housekeeper in a hotel notices the air conditioning unit isn't working properly, so she takes note of it and makes sure the maintenance crew gets word. While it's not her job to take care of the AC or notify maintenance, she takes a few extra bites of responsibility to create value for everyone. If you adopt that mentality, it gives you the opportunity to pay more attention to what's happening around you. Not only must you keep tuned in to what's going on, but you also have to be willing to adjust your schedule and embrace interruptions.

A janitor with that perspective might hear a person at the vending machine struggling to get it to work for her. Because he heard her sighs and frustrations, the problem becomes his responsibility. He doesn't work on vending machines. He doesn't even have the key, so he could legitimately say that it wasn't his problem. But a janitor with an ownership mentality takes his broom and walks down the hall to the vending machine to investigate the problem.

He starts with the question, "Is there something I can help with?"

"This machine won't take my dollar."

With no way to get the machine open, what would you do?

The janitor who takes ownership reaches in his pocket and trades her a crisp dollar bill for the one in her hand. Problem averted, and the woman now has a better perception of the entire organization because a man with a broom helped her with an inconsequential thing.

If I'm the manager and I see or hear about what that janitor did, I'm now going to pay more attention to that person. I want to know what he does for us and how he approaches everything else. There's a good chance this man's culture is in alignment with our core values, so we want to keep him. This is the kind of person that you help rachet up or at least give first right of refusal when a job opens that he qualifies for or can be trained in.

The take ownership mentality can be taught; however, when the person doesn't truly understand value and how to maintain perspective, you'll find yourself resorting to incentives, and the results will be moderate. On the other hand, when it comes to the surface as a natural ability, and you don't have to teach it, it is extremely impactful from a value standpoint.

Zeros Are Recession Proof

One of the beautiful positives of the JAAZ methodology is its recession-proof nature. By taking ownership of our future, we can overcome the hurdles presented by recessions, declining markets, layoffs, and downsizing. Some people use those economic facts as excuses. And when you cling to an excuse long enough, it becomes your truth. Instead of owning their future, the downturn owns them.

Regardless of the economy, tomorrow morning billions of people will wake up and leave their house. They will travel from point A to point B, and they'll need countless things to help them along their journey—education, gas, food . . . fill in the blank. With so many people moving to and fro, natural curiosity can put you on the path to progress.

What do these people need? What resources do I have to fill in their blank and reduce the friction in their lives? When you take ownership of your economy, you connect the dots and find a way to create value for a small portion of those billions of people. And because you are unique and your creativity is involved, you have the potential to make something bigger and better than anyone else.

The person who takes ownership sees that even when they grow tired because the economy has made it tough, they have potential. Supply chain issues may force you to reinvent your distribution model. You may lose heart when the world seems to be shutting down. It's time to restate the facts, look for the friction, and remember your passion.

Economic downturn can't take your contacts nor can it touch your wisdom. People armed with JAAZ and an ownership mentality repackage themselves. They start a new business and create a product no one can buy off the shelf. Their competitors become clients. Margin compression is a thing of the past because they no longer have a traditional commodity. And there's a good chance that as you avoided disaster an economy that sucked in those who couldn't restate the facts, you added several zeros to your opportunity.

How Anyone Can Take Ownership

Your first step in taking ownership, may be a change in mindset. The primary shift will be rejecting the societal norms of passing blame along with the other extreme of false humility. People who refuse to admit when they've made a mistake cannot use the mess as a learning opportunity. In the same hand, feigning modesty impedes progress as well. If people believe you didn't take part in the process, they don't know where to go with questions that can move the project forward.

Owners pinpoint their unique abilities and make them known to others so that their teams can perform as efficiently as possible. Owners become leaders as they share even the craziest idea because they know someone else might be able to connect the dots and turn the crazy into amazing.

Pursuing the why and maintaining perspective remain the first two steps in adding zeros. Ideas that come without pursuing the why serve no one. And leaders who forget to look at projects from every angle, including the view of those they serve and those they work with, become arrogant and unproductive.

After you've learned to pursue the why, maintain perspective, and take ownership, FILM (Friction Identification that Leverages the Market) can be a reality. But nothing adds zeros like including others in the win.

CHAPTER 5

Win Together

Happiness, cannot be pursued; it must ensue, and it only does so as the unintended side effect of one's personal dedication to a cause greater than oneself or as the by-product of one's surrender to a person other than oneself.
—Viktor Frankl

B Y NOW YOU'VE FIGURED out that a big part of the JAAZ philosophy boils down to creating value for others. As you use your natural curiosity to explore the why, you will always find ways to ease friction for you personally. But I don't feel like that's the right option. Anytime I discover that the solution gives me an advantage over the other person involved in a business deal, I know it's not the right fit. My goal is to create a win for everyone.

If you stop and allow your curiosity to find a way for you and your connection to share the profits or balance the benefit, you will always win. You might not make as much as if you worked the plan to tip the scale in your favor; however, when you identify a way that allows you to work together and help the other person make just a little more, you'll find that over time you'll see a bigger revenue.

Conversely, if you constantly manipulate things so you get a bigger payoff, you're like a car with a bad tire. The bad tire seems like it's always winning the battle because the car will pull in that direction—eventually, you will find yourself in a ditch. And I don't know about you, but I don't want to end up with a business that's in a ditch.

To bring the zeros to reality, we have to connect the dots between our curiosity, capability, and connections. And to expand to our fullest potential, we also connect the dots for others to create collaboration. The more value we bring to other people, the fuller our life will be, and the more growth we'll be able to create.

Recognize Your Reach

If you're willing to maintain integrity and provide value, every time you begin a new enterprise, you'll have built-in clients. When people trust you, and see that you want the best for them, they gravitate your way.

By meeting contractors, farmers, and car dealers on their turf, I became the number one phone guy in those industries. When I began to add a zero to my company by offering to analyze billing statements every month for a small per-line fee, my Nextel customers, as well as their referrals, wanted to work with me. After all, who are you going to buy phones from, the guy who signs you up and never looks back, or the person who looks at your bill every month and saves you money? It didn't take long for my business to begin scaling faster than I could handle.

The friction of not being able to keep up with growth looks like a good problem to have from the outside looking in, but the pressure can be overwhelming. It causes a number of businesses to falter. Owners begin to work so many hours they burn out. You might say they've lost control. They don't own the business. The business owns them.

FILM must kick in. Friction Identification sees the problem and understands that utilizing their reach will allow the entrepreneur to take back their company, share the win with another small business, and Leverage the Market.

In my case, I recognized I couldn't train a crew fast enough to keep up, so I connected with a couple of software engineers. I asked them, "If I can give you all the business logic of how I analyze these phone bills, could you create an app that would do the work for me?"

And just like that, a few years before the iPhone™ came out, I used my reach, and started a software company. You might think the owner of a software company understands basic coding. However, while I recognize code for applications, I have no idea how to write it. I don't need to—I know people who can. Plus, I know people who need the code. Recognizing my reach and connecting the dots allows me to provide value and add zeros for myself, the software engineers, and my clients.

As I mentioned earlier, starting the software company because I needed to solve the friction of a business scaling faster than I could keep up with sent me looking for ways to solve friction for my HVAC customers. These business owners didn't even know they had friction, but I'll say it again, solving one point of friction creates more friction. And it's not always a bad thing.

Blackberry came into the mainstream about this time, relieving all kinds of friction for businesses and opening the door for natural curiosity. I noticed that my service provider clients had no way to communicate with the technicians in the field.

What if HVAC companies could schedule their technicians in real time, give them directions to their next appointment and allow the technicians to start sending invoices the moment they completed the project? Could this new technology allow these same technicians to inventory their trucks and put those pieces of inventory on the invoice when they used it? With software engineers already in place, and the power of the why and natural curiosity driving me, I began to contemplate the impact mobile browsers could have on the companies I serve.

So, I made an appointment with the executives at Blackberry and painted my vision. There in the basement of their offices in Toronto, I shared my plan. As far as they were concerned, I was just a dealer from Charlotte, North Carolina; however, they could see I was delivering solutions. They recognized we had the capability to make their product even more impactful than they had seen, and I became the first official Blackberry dealer in uptown Charlotte.

Software engineers in my company took my vision and created an app for the HVAC service guys to clock in and out. Next, each truck became a profit center with the Blackberry phone as the point of information. They used the Blackberry to book and keep track of appointments, create and send invoices, and manage inventory. Clients who used this new service were able to get paid sooner and save valuable time for their accounting department. In fact, those technicians could take payments through the application we created. Long before any remote point-of-sale applications had been developed, our clients received payments immediately instead of thirty days or more after billing.

After I saw how this benefited the HVAC industry, my software company adapted the program for other clients. Our company began building apps for other companies and with each one, we added zeros.

This is just one example of our win together experience. The software engineers added a zero every time someone purchased the app, the clients added zeros with each dollar they saved, and I added a few zeros because I owned the software company as

> ABOVE ALL ELSE, ALIGN WITH CUSTOMERS. WIN WHEN THEY WIN. WIN ONLY WHEN THEY WIN.
>
> JEFF BEZOS

well as the wireless company. The success of the app made the Blackberry phones even more popular, and it became a win for everyone.

As you begin to consider your own reach, just look around. Your reach begins in your backyard. It includes your baseball team and moms' circle, the small group at church as well as your fantasy football league. Anyplace you gather with other people—physically or virtually—gives you reach. Plus, when you create value for you and the other person you touch, you add zeros financially, with regards to integrity, and because the person now begins to send referrals, you add zeros to your reach.

Leverage the Friction

By creating a win-together environment, you can pinpoint friction that will help you leverage the market. Nextel did it by creating a push-to-talk phone. When we purchased those for our staff at the western shop, I didn't have to meet every delivery truck or be on the customer's site when we delivered. With the click of a button, my guys could give me a beep-beep and ask where I wanted a trailer dropped or the load stacked. Because the creators of Nextel saw friction and found a way to solve it, I had more time to connect dots and give my patrons and staff a win.

One of my favorite ways to leverage the market is through recurring income. After the first few times I found out how to provide value through subscription services and receive a check every month for something I had created earlier, I knew I didn't want to lug around fifty-pound bags of feed for the rest of my life.

I have helped numerous entrepreneurs leverage the friction in their company and industry. One such relationship began early one Tuesday. A gentleman I met when delivering phones and training on Blackberry use called. He was launching a siding company to service production home builders and asked if we could discuss their technology needs. Over the next several years, the SeedSpark flywheel helped his organization grow at a very high percentage rate, ultimately becoming the largest organization in their category in the entire US. We did this by meeting them exactly where they were—the beginning—and focusing on how they could apply JAAZ to their thinking. They placed a lot of trust in me and SeedSpark. Every ninety days we met and mapped out ways to leverage the friction continuously created by the growth driven by Just Add a Zero thinking. The payoff was immense. After eight years of Removing the FILM and applying JAAZ, the organization sold for hundreds of millions.

One way for a business to truly leverage friction and grow enterprise value is move from a project-based model to a subscription. I love to study project-based businesses and uncover ways to repackage them to make recurring income. You have a manufacturing business. How can you turn that into a subscription service? Most people think they could never turn that kind of company into recurring income, but I've done it about twenty-five times. I find a lot of fun in taking the most unlikely project-based business and helping repackage it.

How Can I Make Myself Better?

If infinite is better, then you, too, can become infinitely better. Every experience in life, each thing you learn—whether it's from a positive or negative means—can catapult you into something better.

> MY LIFE IS AN EXACT REFLECTION OF MY CHOICES, WHEN I'M BORN, I LOOK LIKE MY PARENTS. WHEN I DIE, I LOOK LIKE MY CHOICES. YOU BECOME WHAT YOU REPEAT.

Too often, people settle for growing vertically. They become the best at what they do; however, their existence is extremely one dimensional. Businesses can fall prey to this pitfall as well. For instance, Kodak™ stayed so narrowly focused on film photography that even though they created the first self-contained digital camera, they dismissed its value and fell from the number one brand in the industry to almost unknown. Believe it or not, Xerox® created the first personal computer; however, their management team thought paper copies would always beat out digital. Blockbuster allowed Netflix® to outpace them, and Blackberry, though they led mobile technology at their onset, concerned themselves with protecting intellectual property to the extent they failed to adapt to changes. MySpace™, Commodore, AoL, and Polaroid® are all foreign words to the current generation despite their innovative starts. All fell into that vertical, one-dimensional mindset.

On the other hand, I recently talked to a man who remembers being hired at age twenty-six to oust the fifty-six-year-old in the corporation. Twenty-seven years later, he's the guy the company has added to their downsize list; however, unlike his predecessor, this man has been expanding himself horizontally. He knows more about the company than any other person there. Every department has felt his influence, and after they let him go, this individual will likely become their consultant. They'll pay him five times what he made while he was on the payroll, and if they don't hire him, one of their competitors will.

For nearly three decades, this man has been reading, examining, soaking in every bit of information. The corporation who thinks they can hire a younger, less expensive executive has a value mismatch. This man has become infinitely better and increased his value exponentially. He can name his price because the revenue his wisdom will bring will far outweigh what they pay him. Though the day of his exit from the corporate world is inevitable, he now gets to control that exit.

One-dimensional fifty-seven-year-olds will find themselves in a much different position. No matter what organization you are in, it will either go in a different direction or decline; regardless, your job will be gone. Maintaining a growth mindset that constantly tries to better yourself has the innate capability of stretching you horizontally. Add time, and you will find yourself with vertical expertise.

It's a recalibration of our minds. Rather than thinking our jobs are in jeopardy because they pay us too much, we need to understand that they really aren't paying us what we're worth. The company won't realize it until they begin paying us the consultant's fee. And if we manage to recognize our value ten years before the company decides to replace us, we ensure we never have to face that day.

Instead, we take the expertise they paid us to create, use it to implement innovative ideas for the industry, then turn around and sell it back to them. By making ourselves infinitely better, we put ourselves in the catbird seat, but not only do we win, many other companies benefit because we can spread our horizontal knowledge and vertical expertise throughout the industry.

Who Does This Benefit?

Pursuing the why means also asking who. Who will my innovation benefit? As I said at the beginning of this chapter, if the only person who gains from my ideas is me, then it's not an idea I want to implement. First, it's not the kind of business I want to run. I enjoy seeing people succeed. Second, it limits my ability to add zeros.

When you come into business with a mindset of helping someone, everything else takes care of itself. I live by the philosophy you must give to get.

> HAPPINESS CANNOT BE ATTAINED BY WANTING TO BE HAPPY—IT MUST COME AS THE UNINTENDED CONSEQUENCE OF WORKING FOR A GOAL GREATER THAN ONESELF.
> FRED KOFMAN

I've met salespeople whose main objective is to market a product. I immediately tell them they don't want to do it that way. Instead, I encourage them to put themselves in their ideal customer's shoes. How can you help them accomplish their goals, and how will the product you want to provide add zeros to their bottom line?

I enter every conversation with a mindset that says, "How can I create value for this company?" Never, and I mean never, do I try to sell them something. I don't look at these people as clients but as collaborators. I see their business as my own. This means our conversations create an enormous amount of confidence, and these companies want to do business with me because there is an immediate trust built in for my capability to provide for them. As Simon Sinek puts it, "People don't buy what you do, they buy why you do it."

Each member of my team embraces this same philosophy. They take their purview and their experience and use them to find ways to potentially help the person they are talking to. They begin to see each person on my staff as the person who brings solutions. The customer may understand the basics of my staff member's responsibilities, but because he or she has created a relationship and provided value, my staff member becomes the hero.

When a marketing firm contacted us to discuss options for growing the market share for one of their premier clients, we saw an opportunity to implement the SeedSpark Flywheel. This company provided parts internationally for airlines, school systems, state agencies, and more. Their unique collaborative approach meant they had already mastered one of the key components of the FlyWheel-Growth Through Collaboration. They already had over one hundred years of successful business growth and were ready to leverage the friction.

We went to work and created an application that automated their usage and distribution reviews. This simple shift facilitated growth into over forty new markets across the US and Canada. They requested some out-of-the-box thinking and received a reporting tool able to add more than just one zero. Never let the request dictate the value you can create. JAAZ thinking often means pulling the small string to move an entire mountain. We don't focus on the size of the accomplishment; we always steer our thinking to the value we can create.

Whenever you collaborate with someone with the goal of providing a much bigger outcome for the other person, you will indirectly win too. The trust you build by using your expertise to bring value means you have a returning customer with glowing referrals. You will scale faster than you could ever imagine simply because you focused on helping someone else win.

When we turn our focus to giving instead of receiving, the rest kind of takes care of itself. Our activity will have a measure of hustle, but it will be energy we put in rather than what we can hustle out of them.

How Anyone Can Use the Win Together Principle

When you begin to implement this mindset change, it will take a little bit of time. But if you're committed to it, it does happen, and you end up with control over your destiny.

The key to winning together is shifting your mindset to always looking for profitability for yourself and others. We start to think bigger than our own little problems. The mindset shifts to "How can fixing my problem fix someone else's problem?"

One intern I mentored lived this principle. He took ownership of any and everything that crossed his path. Within six months of shadowing me, the young man was earning six figures as a college student. All because he embodied these core values. He always asked great questions. He pursued the why until he found the answer. A champion at maintaining perspective, clients loved him. His win-together approach not only took ownership of every problem and success he came to, it caused him to naturally help the client see the project through to the end. He made certain the client had a win even if he had little interest in it. How did that manifest for him? It took him straight to the top.

The win-together strategy doesn't work without using natural curiosity to pursue the why, looking at life through the eyes of the client, and taking ownership of the details, so when he excelled in all four, he couldn't be stopped. Anyone who works to make sure everyone wins together can see the same success. And the same can be true of you.

CHAPTER 6

Curiosity + Capability + Connections = Collaboration

Alone we can do so little; together we can do so much.

—Helen Keller

THESE FOUR CORE VALUES have allowed me to connect the dots, apply the FILM, and use the JAAZ methodology across a variety of companies. Friction Identification enables me to do what I love—help others succeed. And when a particular innovation works for more than one business, I Leverage the Market and create a new company around that idea. Plus, because I've built trust among the people I work with, if this new business serves their needs, I automatically have new clients. I've started and sold many enterprises, and I maintain ownership of even more endeavors that provide value to my connections.

The Just Add a Zero philosophy is a big spiral upwards with no end. Curiosity added to capability coupled with connections allows me to see and create collaborations that offer more opportunity to use my natural curiosity to use my capabilities and connections to create more collaborations. It has a Möbius quality.

A Möbius is created when a rectangular strip gets an odd number of half twists and then its ends are joined. If you follow the strip from start to finish, you will touch every inch of both sides of the strip. Psychologists believe it represents the thought and the unthought all in one artistic shape. It's an unorientable configuration with no definable up or down, in or out. It has depth, and rather than circular, it's dynamic.[10] That's JAAZ thinking. It's out-of-the-box, multidimensional, and has no beginning or end.

The Möbius of Collaboration

The best collaborations are like the Möbius—out-of-the-box, multidimensional, and unlimited. While the Ford Motor Company didn't officially start its designer-line Lincolns until the mid-70s, Edsel Ford began a personal relationship with Cartier decades before. The basic Model T Ford didn't require much design, but Edsel wanted the Lincoln line to be different. "Father wanted to make the most popular car," the younger Ford stated, "I wanted to make the best." As Edsel discussed his ideas with a most unlikely car collaborator, he discovered a compa-

JUST ADD A ZERO

ny that specializes in extraordinary jewelry and watches could help him reach his goal.

When Ford introduced the Lincoln designer series, unheard of advancements appeared in the cars. Metal interiors became covered with leather, cloth, and vinyl. Gold plating covered even the keys. Later on, as they added a Bill Blass line to the Mustang and Givenchy and Pucci to their designer cars, the famous automobile company started hosting festivals for the designers. Brand historian Ted Ryan described these launches. "The introduction of each new designer edition became something like a fashion line being premiered in Paris or New York."[11]

Few would have predicted the collaboration of a jeweler and a car manufacturer, yet their union transformed the entire car industry. Like the Möbius, the design morphed with each turn, but never ended. And the concept has a repeatable and equally profitable process if we choose to embrace it.

Every Meeting Is an Opportunity

When Edsel Ford met the top executives at Cartier, he didn't plan on creating a designer line. He and the Cartier brothers shared a common goal, to make things better. They corresponded often, and Ford ordered all his business cards and stationery from the jewelry giant. Though evidence of their connection dates to the early 1920s, the business collaboration didn't begin until forty-five years later.

Just Add a Zero thinking sees every meeting as an opportunity. Regardless of the quality of the encounter, it can add something to your life. Every business and person I meet creates an imprint on my brain. I remember where they're from, their hobbies, interests, and unique abilities. My occipital lobe shares this imprint with the memory portion of my mind. One day, in another unexpected meeting, I will see a hole in that entrepreneur's organization, a space that the previous organizations capabilities or reach can fill just right, and I recommend a collaboration. The more people I meet, the bigger the database of connections at my disposal to create collaborations that drive exponential growth.

I live in the belief that I can learn something from everyone, and every connection has potential. This mindset has allowed me to expand my horizons beyond anyone's imagination as well as help catapult others to exponential success.

My brain naturally retains information about people. You, on the other hand, may need to use your capabilities differently. This digital age we live in gives you a huge advantage over your grandparents. CRMs, AI-powered note-taking programs, and indexed, searchable files offer places to store and recall information about every encounter. Then as your vision grows and your reach expands, you can explore these past connections. You will discover a myriad of ways to connect the dots in your lists, adding zeros for you and your connections.

With each win you create, you'll find you've also added yourself to someone else's mental database. Like trying to find the end of the Möbius strip, the opportunities will begin to overlap. Clients from one endeavor will become clients in another. With many of my clients, I began as the horse trailer and feed guy. Now, I help them reach success in almost every area of their business. They call me for referrals, consulting, and more—all because I understand the importance of these relationships and the potential they have to help me connect the dots and add zeros.

Not About the Business or the Model

Too many businesses are laser-focused on their business model. However, as Simon Sinek says, "People don't buy what you do; they buy why you do it." Sinek uses Apple as an example. Apple has a goal to challenge the status quo, and those who love new technology resonate with that why. How you approach your business and who you do it with makes a difference.

As I help entrepreneurs use their curiosity to find their capability, connections, and collaborations, I encourage them to focus on their vision, capability, and reach.

When I look backwards over my life, I see horses, animal feed, trailers, gates, phones, software, data centers, leasing, real estate, manufacturing, and all the other things I've had my hands on over the years. In order to figure out my true business capability, I have to ask myself, "What is the common thread in everything I've experienced?"

In my case, from the moment I realized what my father made each year to my most recent business encounter, I understand my unique ability is to see the middle, where the good stuff is, in between two resources. And by good stuff I mean things that once identified and collaborated with create value resulting in exponential growth. I honestly prefer to stay in an industry just long enough to uncover the solution to their problem of friction, create value, and pass it along. I call it uncovering the how so I can sell it to the whos.

That's what gives me the edge. Providing value transcends business models and types. It offers an opportunity to get inside every company—not to recreate their product or service as some might imagine. No, it's an opportunity to get inside and identify the things they are creating that are special and unique—things no one else sees. It allows me to empower these entrepreneurs to change the game and increase their value proposition.

Despite business model myths, you don't have to be an industry expert to provide value. In fact, I think my lack of expertise may be a key ingredient of my secret sauce. I have no preconceived conventions, my natural curiosity takes over, Friction Identification engages, and I see ways for the person I'm conversing with to Leverage the Market and Just Add A Zero through collaborations. The key will always be looking for ways to create value rather than just creating a better business.

Add a Zero to the Facts

When we engage our curiosity, capabilities, and connections, we can bring together a collaboration that will exponentially change the facts. For instance, supply chain issues and the market forced one of my projects into about 25 percent

> THERE IS ONE GRAND
> LIE—THAT WE ARE
> LIMITED. THE ONLY
> LIMITS WE HAVE
> ON OURSELVES ARE
> THE ONES THAT
> WE BELIEVE.
> WAYNE W. DYER

overruns. The initial investment was larger than typical, so each investor just waited on everyone else to be the first to put in the extra funds.

It would have been easy to look at the bare facts and see the enormity of the extra investment. However, when we added a zero to the facts, we saw the bigger picture. The same issues that demanded the extra investment increased the final value of the project. The projected income promised to be greater than we'd put in the original forecast.

Those who chose to focus on the single negative fact—an expensive overrun—missed the facts that add zeros. On the other hand, those who took a step back and broke down the anatomy of the potential opportunity saw a return within nine months of launching the project. In fact, we had a potential to double our money in just a year.

Unfortunately, too many investors have only one question: "What's required of me?" This requirement mindset sets limits. Fear keeps them from moving ahead. Natural curiosity drives the opportunistic mentality, so there are an unlimited number of questions to feed the zeros.

Rather than "what is," natural curiosity asks "what if" and "why." By examining the facts from the perspective of what am I able to do rather than what do I have to do, we see the potential. The "what do I have to do" mindset saw the increased investment. The "what if I made the investment" perspective recognized a significant return in a short period of time.

When we add a zero to the facts, we take apart the timelines, reconnecting and associating them in ways the normal mind doesn't understand. Years ago, when the construction market saw a huge decline, builders in my area had to drop their prices, and they put pressure on their vendors to cut their pricing. This would mean layoffs, decreased revenue, and hardship all around.

At the time, I was the Nextel provider for most of the landscaping companies in the metropolitan area, and I entertained a proposition for them. I made no money on the deal, but I helped them add a zero by adopting an opportunistic mindset during a very difficult financial time.

I explained that if they all came together as a consortium of sorts and held fast on their pricing, they could keep their employees and maintain their market share. They knew when the economy rebounded, this arrangement would dissolve, but they temporarily collaborated for their common good. By looking at what was possible instead of what the contractors required, they lived to fight another day.

Change Creates Opportunity

These landscapers recognized the market had shifted, and while the contractors were struggling to breathe, the landscapers embraced opportunity.

The market is continually changing, and with every move, we see pressure in pricing. Those who live in the required mindset resist the change, but in order to add zeros, you have to face reality, and you have to choose the lens through which you view it.

Those who fight the shift because they don't like being forced to make adjustments will flounder, and some will fail. But those who embrace the improv will be able to dance.

It's a matter of seeing the change as untapped potential. Rather than saying, "Poor me," the opportunistic mindset says, "This is awesome." These individuals embrace what happens in the market or the messes in their industry. When they discover a piece of equipment or a part to repair their machines is being discontinued, they grab hold of the opportunity.

When we recast the facts to see obstacles as opportunity, we'll see the shift in mindset creates a shift in market share because while we're all running to the right to seize the potential that lies in the unknown, our competition has gathered in fear on the left.

Whether it's a recession, government shutdown, supply chain issues, a change in parts, or something more devastating, the mindset that sees change as potential opportunity will always succeed. The required mindset will struggle during those shifts because they're looking through the lens of the status quo. They won't even see those difficult times coming for them.

Part Three: Clarity

CHAPTER 7

Zeros Outside the Box

The more you pursue meaning, the more money pursues you.

—Lee Brower

THE JUST ADD A Zero methodology is outside-the-box thinking at its finest. A conventional mindset will miss the friction and never ask questions. So many people go through training sessions and regurgitate the same information day after day. They complain about the status quo, but they never ask the questions that can make the change.

Conventional thinking sees a contract ending. Out-of-the-box thinking sees an opportunity to dig a little deeper. Why is the contract ending? Often, the answer allows him to provide a new service, up the stakes, and solve friction.

But when you begin to ask why—Why do we do this that way? Why does this number go in this box?—we find more efficient ways to operate. And in doing so, we add zeros everywhere.

Add a Zero on Both Ends

Adding a zero on the back side of any proposition makes perfect sense. If I make ten dollars today, but I want to look for ways to add a zero, I consider things that will take my enterprise to one hundred dollars. Sometimes when I shoot for one hundred, I'll only make eighty, but before the add-a-zero thinking, I only expected ten or twelve dollars. Exponential thinking always brings growth.

But what happens if you add a zero to the front of your number, and why would you want to do that? Sometimes, we need to cut expenses. In order to add a zero to the back, we often must add a zero to the front. For example, your processes become so efficient that you don't need ten salespeople. You really need eight, but if you use the add-a-zero philosophy, you force yourself to come up with a better idea that will take you to one.

Someone just read that and panicked because their first thought was downsizing; however, in a win-together organization, with a take ownership core value, instead of downsizing, the idea of staff reduction just caused more friction. Now I have to ask, "How can those staff members and I win together?" And the staff starts asking, "How can we take ownership, create value, and add zeros?"

Adding zeros that cause contraction rather than ␣␣␣ sion seems counterproductive to most people. However, it forces questions no one ever asks and results in greater impact. How can reduction bring an increase? Even adding zeros to the end causes you to think differently than the rest of the world because they're thinking in ones and you're considering magnification.

Anytime you can take your thinking outside of the box, you have an advantage the average person can't see. By adding reduction to your arsenal of adding zeros, you will set yourself apart and eliminate your competition.

Adjacently Possible

Most people can relate to lateral pattern recognition. It starts in the past. Because of things that happened previously, we can predict what will happen in the future. Meteorologists use it. I can appreciate many aspects of lateral pattern recognition because following the patterns shows us future things we can't see yet. However, I get more excited about non-lateral or adjacent pattern recognition. I love seeing the way things that run next to each other connect, rather than how the events of the past will predictably connect to what will be. I guess I find adventure in the unpredictable.

When I talk to people, I listen to what they say and, eventually, I see patterns in even the most abstract things. Two businesses run down tracks side by side. They each deliver

...d products. What happens when you

d Revenue Versus Recurring Reve...

I have a difficult time getting excited about project-based businesses. Not that I don't appreciate how those trips around the arena on horseback or those hours hogging provided a means for me to grow to where I am now. However, I don't want tomorrow to simply repeat yesterday. I search out new and exciting opportunities in every relationship.

My first taste of recurring revenue came in the form of boarding horses. I had a steady monthly income with a minimal amount of labor involved. Examining phone plans monthly, especially after I collaborated with the software guys to create the app, also let me experience ways to make a living that allowed me to get up every morning and pursue something new.

On the other end of the scale, my most unpleasant experience with recurring revenue occurred as I started selling phones. As I mentioned, Nextel insisted that I run my sales through a dealer in a small nearby town. When they gave me my own dealership, I realized that guy a few miles down the road was keeping my residuals. I should have been getting a few dollars every month from every phone I sold.

From that moment on, I made sure I was always in control of my own recurring income.

Out of that friction, courtesy of that small-town Nextel dealer, I've come up with many ideas that have helped me as well as countless other businesses. I now specialize in creating companies and methodologies that help my clients create their own recurring revenue streams as well as immense enterprise value. I could easily talk about what that dealer did to me two decades ago. But did he do it to me or for me? By restating the facts and maintaining perspective, recurring revenue and my rinse-and-repeat methodology have become such a part of my life that my friends jokingly call me "The King of Recurring."

With so many ideas for improvement constantly floating around my head, I get excited when I find recurring revenue streams. These give me more time to pursue the why and let my natural curiosity assist others in their journey. And I enjoy helping others turn their project-based revenue into recurring income.

The key is focusing on a way to provide value over and over again rather than just one time. Foundationally, I'll make a large investment of time and then, over time, I'll see the return on that investment. It requires an intentional friction identification and a repeatable solution. Then when I exit the business, it will be worth up to fifteen times more than the project-based endeavor.

More than a Product or Service

Conventional thinking tells us if we have the highest quality product or service or the best price, we should have the most successful business. Experience tells us this isn't always the case. I've seen more than one exceptional company experience huge losses when the whims of their customers changed.

The key to the Just Add A Zero philosophy is focusing on the ones we serve. When we ask questions and continue to pursue the why until we feel satisfied with the answer, we can uncover friction and help our customers scale. The people we

> YOU CAN HAVE EVERYTHING IN LIFE YOU WANT, IF YOU WILL JUST HELP ENOUGH OTHER PEOPLE GET WHAT THEY WANT.
> ZIG ZIGLAR

work with need to know we are always listening, seeing friction from their point of view, and putting their interests ahead of our own.

One of the principles that I've taught my girls is to always find a compliment. I remind them each year when they return to school to find one compliment every day. Imagine how they stand out when they tell their teachers, "I like that blouse." "Those are pretty earrings." Compliments tell people we're paying attention, and they make them feel good. We create value by being authentic.

Out-of-the-box thinking adds as many zeros to the clients as it adds to itself. I believe in the name your price premise;

however, that basically means you can control your income. If you charge unfairly and are simply looking for ways to line your own pocket, the JAAZ methodology won't work for you.

You may be the best at what you do and offer it at the most affordable price; however, if a similar provider is constantly looking for ways to solve friction for your customer, they'll take your lunch. You won't even see it coming.

Just Add a Zero means Friction Identification to Leverage the Market for you as well as your client. When you add that mindset to exceptional products and service, you'll become unstoppable. And when you keep that perspective, you'll discover that winning together is the only way to do business.

Name Your Price

Conventional mindsets are constantly worried about minimum wage and cutting the competition. On the other end of that conventional spectrum, you'll have price gougers and people who think name your price means taking advantage of others.

Out-of-the-box thinking understands that naming your price means taking control of your income. At the same time, when you change the rules, you remove margin compression. For example, my friend who collaborated with Lowe's® and The Home Depot® made it easier for both companies to do business with him over other companies.

He's scaled to become viewed as a business partner because he is constantly helping remove the friction for these big box stores in his specialty areas.

The level of trust he built with these other CEOs allowed him to influence the amount all service providers received. He has made himself irreplaceable and created competitive advantages that enable him to set his price. When they ask my friend to go into a new market, he does the studies and runs it through his program because he's discovered ways to take all the fat out of the process. He's able to deliver efficiently and leverage a better price as he enters the new market. Many times, when he's offered a new market, it's because the current provider isn't up to snuff. So, even if his price comes in higher, he's in the catbird seat. He will make a little money—a win for him—and he will deliver the product with an excellent level of service—a win for the big box store.

Naming your price doesn't mean charging whatever you want. It means embracing the core values that allow you to win together. To name your price, you use natural curiosity to pursue the why. "Why are they paying their current price?" "What will it cost me?" By maintaining your customer's perspective throughout the conversation and taking ownership of your price as well as your client's best interest, you can have a real exchange that will allow you to keep and maintain your margin. Setting your own price will always be governed by the value you can provide. On the other hand, you don't have to settle for a low margin just because everyone else in the industry does it.

When you change the game by providing quality and value different than anyone else is doing it, you now have no competition, and you can set your own price.

CHAPTER 8

What's Next

Start where you are. Use what you have. Do what you can.

—Arthur Ashe

A FTER ALL THIS, YOU might be thinking, *Where do I begin?* I would answer, "Begin where you are."

First, take inventory of your resources. What kinds of things do you have at your disposal? I started with a horse, then a tractor and a bush hog.

Next, create a list of your capabilities, and don't dismiss any as insignificant. Where have you provided value for past employers or your family and friends?

Finally, consider your connections. Who should be in your inner circle? Which of those connections needs moved out a ring or two and who should you be spending more time with?

Now take those lists and begin asking the questions. How can I use my resources and capabilities to provide value? Why do the people on my list do the things they do, and what would happen if I helped them see things differently?

Too often, I meet business owners and entrepreneurs with great intentions. They'll take action as soon as they pass some milestone or meet an arbitrary goal. If we want to add zeros, we have to remember—the future always starts now. Those words Squire Bill Widener told Teddy Roosevelt, "Do what you can, with what you have, where you are."[12] became a foundational outline for one of my core views. We have all we ever need to get started. We simply need to identify and leverage ourselves, our abilities, and our immediate resources .

In its infancy, Just Add a Zero thinking begins wherever you are right the moment. It takes an account of all the things you think need improved and how much improvement is required. Before you take any action, you consistently force yourself to ask, "What would this look like if it was ten times better?"

Now you can circle back to your resources. These may seem small, but when you combine them, you can create great things. *What if I used resource A with resource B?* No matter how unlikely the pairing, if the two resources create value by working together, you now have a collaboration of sorts, and you'll begin to see the increase.

Dean Jackson of the *I Love Marketing* podcast shared three words with me—vision, capability, and reach. He says everyone has at least one of these in abundance and probably more than one. It's a matter of changing our mindset to see our resources, capabilities, and connections as assets. Only after you recognize the value of these three items can you use them to pass the value on to others.

Let's say you use your capabilities to create something of value for those folks in your backyard, the ones we discussed in chapter 5. You now can start a small business because you shared your capabilities with your reach to add value to their lives. This is the first layer of Just Add a Zero thinking.

To create another layer, rinse, and repeat—understand your resources, create value, and look for reach. Every time natural curiosity shows you how to put more of these assets together, you create new value and minor collaborations until one day you discover in order to add another zero, you need to bring on a person who is better in one of the areas that you don't excel in.

Perhaps you have tremendous vision. Your natural curiosity allows you to see and solve friction like no one else you know. You have the idea as well as the connections that can benefit from it. Next, you identify a collaboration partner with a unique capability to build the product. By adding this layer of collaboration, you can now bring so much value that people you've never met before want to work with you—all because you adjusted your mindset to recognize your vision, capability, and reach and allowed your natural curiosity to ask the right questions.

Make It Easy for People to Do Business with You

Successful JAAZ entrepreneurs have one major thing in common. They make it easy for people to do business with them. We've already established that JAAZ involves improv, and building a business with exponential growth does too.

When I started selling Nextel phones, every other dealer had a storefront you could visit to set up your accounts. My natural curiosity explored the habits of my clients and asked the question, "What would make it easier for these folks to do business with me?" They were busy, and especially in the case of contractors, multiple crafts were gathered in one place. When I began to visit job sites, farms, and car dealerships, I became the natural choice among the area's cell phone providers. When landscapers realized I was willing to go to their offices before their trucks left for the morning, they wanted to do business with me. Even if I had charged more, the convenience would have been worth it.

This meant that when I offered to check their statement every month to make certain they were getting the best deal, they were even more anxious to sign up.

The questions of natural curiosity will give you the information you need to make your company's practices different than others. You'll start to think outside the box, and your innovations will eliminate the competition because you don't do things the way everyone else does. Most importantly, more people will want to work with you.

Every time you adjust to make it easy for people to do business with you, you'll add zeros for yourself as well as your current clients, and you'll give them a reason to send others your way.

Create Something Replicable

One of the secrets of Just Add A Zero is its rinse-and-repeat capability. If you can create a system that others can use to get similar success, you can sell or lease your process. The replicable nature of Just Add a Zero becomes a never-ending spiral of friction reduction. Seldom will you solve friction for one person that isn't being felt by another. In any given business or service area, there's a good chance they are encountering obstacles similar to those in other unrelated businesses.

When you begin to pursue the why and identify the root of the friction, you have opened the door to create a process to alleviate that problem for many others.

I'm working with a gentleman who is a service provider for residential assisted living facilities. Unfortunately, in his state, they've opened the door for tons and tons of service providers into the arena. Consequently, the market is saturated with unqualified, horribly staffed providers who can't deliver anything close to the excellence this gentleman provides.

The reason that he's been able to grow and excel at what he does is that he has a system to take any average person and train them in his process, and their success makes him look like a hero.

The state had created real friction by allowing sub-standard providers to work for them, but this gentleman has a replicable solution. What if he presented it to the state and they accepted it? This would mean all those unqualified providers would become his clients as he begins to sell them his system to meet the state's standards. I concede that in four years, his enterprise will have created so much value that he can leave the residential assisted living business and either have recurring income from his system or sell the platform for a nice profit.

By looking around and seeing friction, he created a plan that can be easily replicable. It provides value for him as well as those he serves, and it adds zeros all around.

Be the Guy that Connects the Dots

If you're willing to develop your natural curiosity and put it to work for you, you can be the guy that connects the dots. It starts with you. Always begin by doing what you can with what you have where you are. How can you connect your resources and capabilities? What do you see in your immediate environment—things you thought could never connect—that you could bring together to create more value?

Many of my first connections involved hard work. For instance, the barn that allowed me to rent stable space was only available because I had to get the building process started and set every post before I could go to the beach with the family. I was only a teen at the time, and it involved a lot of grit and determination. I joined my resources with my capabilities to add value to my dad's farm; however, it didn't take long for it to add zeros in my life when I began to use the barn myself.

After you begin to add zeros in your own life, you can add layers outside yourself. It begins by asking, "How can I add value to the lives of these people I'm already serving?" Those horses were already in my barn. Natural curiosity encouraged me to consider my capabilities and give my boarding clients a new option. For another fee, I could train their horses while they were in my care. The horse owners loved knowing they'd get a trained horse back after leaving it with me for a month, and I added zeros.

Today I use the same principle as I add even more layers. For instance, I can't code, and the guys who can code don't relate well to the businesses, but I have the capabilities and resources to communicate with both. Using natural curiosity and my unique ability, I brought the two together and created zeros for everyone.

The world changes continually, and with every fluctuation, opportunities to connect dots appear as if by magic. But much like those who hear the entire ensemble play and can't pick out the individual instruments, if you aren't looking for and listening for those subtle shifts, you'll miss your chance to add zeros.

Every day, even before I open my eyes, I focus my thoughts on gratitude and prayer to keep my mindset strong. The moment I open my eyes, my brain shifts into high gear looking for ways I can create value for those I already serve as well as those I have yet to serve. That is the fun part. I create impact by serving and bringing value in new and innovative ways. Connecting dots makes me a great conduit. If you're willing to change your perspective and ask the right questions, you too can become a walking Triple Play powered by The D.O.S. Conversation® and utilizing its approach to danger, opportunities, and strengths. I share this mindset with my daughters nearly every day because I believe anyone who adopts this methodology will always have a job, and if the world would look for ways to serve, it would be a whole lot better place.

My Favorite Just Add a Zero Hacks

There are some tips I have added to my life to help me be as productive as possible. I recommend adding at least of few of these to help you add zeros to your life.

Set a bedtime. Long ago, I started sending myself to bed at 8:58 p.m. I wake up naturally between 3:00 and 4:00 a.m. By setting a time a little off from convention, it enables me to remember. Set a time that's your time, not the norm. This will help you go to sleep earlier and empower you to WIN tomorrow.

Raise your hand. By always raising your hand first, you get the most attention from the coach or teacher. You don't need to be nervous because no one remembers what you say. Everyone else is sweating bullets because it is likely what they have to say has already been said. Make yourself memorable to your teachers and coaches.

Change the way you brush your teeth. Jim Kwik turned me on to this. By brushing your teeth with your non-dominant hand, you expand the neuron connections and effectively grow your brain. I need all I can get!

Ask two questions. Your subconscious works twenty-four hours a day; your conscience works twelve to fourteen. So those hours you're sleeping give you an easy way to pick up extra processing time. Be intentional. Just before you go to bed, write two questions on a journal page—one at the top and one at the middle. You may consider writing the date backwards at the top right corner. When you wake and have the answers, record them. You will be amazed at what your brain can do when you are sleeping.

Make your bed. Making your bed allows you to accomplish one thing before others even roll over. Make your bed as soon as you get up in the morning. Sure, this can be tricky with someone else in it. But, so was tying your shoes the first time you tried. This small accomplishment sets you in motion for crushing each and every day.

Keep your eyes closed. I have trained myself to keep my eyes closed for the first moments every day. Often, I have to breathe to get myself centered. The world screams for my brain to make decisions and figure out things the second I open my eyes. So I don't open them until I spend some time being grateful. I remember that many go to sleep and don't wake up. If you start there, you will find that the trouble you face later that day looks a little smaller and is easier to tackle.

Draft your three. I learned The D.O.S. Conversation from Dan Sullivan and modified it to fit my daily routine. Dan's method is tremendously impactful. The focus it provides each day is overwhelming. There is power in this number three combined with Dan's solid thinking tools. Each morning I list:

- one Danger to remove

- one Opportunity to capture

- one Strength to leverage

How Do I Know My Friction Solution Will Work?

One thing that holds people back is the fear that their idea won't work. But what if your friction solution is just the first step in a major breakthrough? Most know that Thomas Edison filed the patent for the first commercially manufactured lightbulb, but he would have had a much more difficult time had it not been for other pioneers who brought their ideas even though they didn't solve the problem.

In 1802, Humphrey Davy introduced the first electric light bulb, but it didn't last long and wasn't cost effective. Not many people have heard of Warren de la Rue, Joseph Swan, Henry Woodward, and Matthew Evans, a few other names associated with electric lights. However, without the work of each of these men, Edison would have been less successful. What if fear had convinced them to hold back their ideas? Where would we be now?

When we have an idea, it's imperative we test it and share it, and that we share it with the right people. Your mother may tell you every idea you bring is brilliant, but what about the check writer? If the person who will be using and investing in the friction solution believes your idea is valid, then you should go for it, and if you can find a second source to give you confirmation, that's even better.

So many businesses fail to launch because they get bogged down in the paperwork of starting a business. Banks want a business plan and a developed business model. Unfortunately, many brilliant friction solvers have no idea what that means. People with tremendous potential get trapped by the formality of everything some other power requires for them to change the trajectory of their life. Rather than taking immediate action by creating value. They let the friction from loan officers halt their ideas.

It's true that you don't really have a business until someone writes a check for your idea. However, revenue will come when you begin to provide value. I started ten to fifteen companies before I figured out how to create those documents. Despite my lack of business savvy, I had a more important asset. I knew how to provide value.

Whether your solution is vertical—designed specifically for the company you work for—or horizontal—something that can impact an entire industry—you must share it. Your innovation may be the solution that ripples throughout the industry or it might never get off the ground. Alternately, you might build on the solution someone else shared. Regardless, your idea could potentially be the beginning of something bigger than you ever imagined, but no one will ever know if you hide behind the worry or the false assumption that you can't fix the friction.

Working with Chad

One of my greatest pleasures, the thing that makes my business a joy rather than a job, is working with people who've caught the Just Add a Zero vision and need a bit of assistance finding the right collaboration. I love helping them discover their friction and giving them suggestions for solving it while we watch for the friction our solution will invariably create. Using my unique ability, which is uncovering opportunities that deliver exponential impact and results by instantaneously connecting dots, in unconventional ways, I create and manage some amazing collaborations.

I've worked in every aspect of business. I've done the hard labor of caring for horses, stringing fence, and hauling bags of feed. During my final years of high school, I started to think I would have a permanent crick in my neck. For hours every day, I watched the bush hog behind the tractor making sure it stayed straight. As I stretched out that pain each evening, I began to understand that wasn't how I wanted to make a living for the rest of my life. On the other hand, the money I made keeping those bank lots cleared put me in a position to start my first business. But better than that, it allowed me to dig deeper. What patterns and cycles did I see while I mowed, and what did I need to do to get off that tractor?

Software, finances, human resources, and discovering personalities and unique abilities in myself as well as those

I meet have all given me insight to connecting dots and collaborating. Everything I've ever done, even attempting to stack way too many bales on the back of a truck and watching half of them fall off, taught me something about myself and gave me an opportunity to put my natural curiosity to work.

One of my collaborators told me that he doesn't think my unique ability description is entirely accurate because I have a huge relationship component that doesn't get mentioned. As I said, I've been paying attention to people and noticing their nuances since my childhood.

I have an innate ability to see voids as well as the people and companies that will fill them. I immediately know that this guy plus this guy equals results and solutions. I can see relationships working before they're formed, and this capability fuels the opportunities I create for myself and others. Seeing the value created in collaborations and the breakthroughs in relationships and businesses as I help form bonds drives me in an unexplainable way. I love being the catalyst that impacts so many businesses and people, and the ripple effect it has on employees and teams gives me immense satisfaction.

Sometimes I forget not everyone thinks the way I do, and the older I get the more I understand the truth. But even in this, I embrace the differences because I can learn so much from each person and their uniqueness.

Kary Oberbrunner gave me a huge compliment when he said, "What extreme athletes are doing on the sports field, Chad Jenkins is helping entrepreneurs do in the boardroom." Like quarterbacks who stay focused on the play and musicians who ignore the audience to bring a beautiful improv, I tend to be able to listen to many voices and sounds in the room and draw out the melody line for businesses. My natural curiosity sees what others miss, but my chief capability is hearing what hasn't been said and then using my connections to bring collaboration.

Some wonder why I'm so persuasive, and I've thought a lot about that. I think the reason people readily accept my suggestions and trust my companies is that by the time I make referrals, especially recommendations for collaborations, I have vetted the connection or the idea at least fifteen different ways. The result of my natural curiosity and the deep investigation it demands is a non-verbal conviction that accompanies my suggestion. By the time advice leaves my mouth, I've run it through patterns and scenarios in my mind, and those I share with can feel my confidence.

I don't sell anything; instead, I make connections. I love discovering collaborations even if I never make a penny from it. My goal is to connect the dots whether I see revenue or not. The payoff comes in trust built. My connections will someday need something that one of my companies can serve, and they'll come to me. I don't need to sell. Serving and solving brings what I need to add zeros.

Right now, I'm using this methodology with businesses to increase the value of their companies exponentially. For a recurring fee, I find the friction, see my client's perspective, and take partial ownership on the growth in value of their business. This way the founder experiences growth but keeps his all his equity. I will continually help them solve friction and scale until they sell their business, then they'll share a portion of the increase in profit since I began working with them. My clients understand that it's in my best interest to scale their business fast, so the recurring annual fee is a good investment. It's just one of the ways I use my triple play to create wins for my business as well as my clients.

My staff and I take those core values, and whenever we come up with a solution, we rinse it through that filter: Pursue the Why, Maintain Perspective, Take Ownership, and Win Together. When you add a zero to both sides of collaboration using those steps, you have something that will stand the test of time and make a LOT of money and provide value to all parties involved. Plus, if you embrace this concept and maintain this perspective throughout your entire life, you will never be stale. Boredom never occurs in the add a zero lifestyle.

My personal flywheel—the thing that powers me—is removing the film, adding zeros, and growth through collaboration. As I engage with companies and employ my flywheel, together we can create their own moonshot.

Their big idea will help them scale to a place with no competition, set their own price, and expand globally.

The Just Add A Zero philosophy is a continuous spiral of Friction Identification and Leveraging the Market. Friction solutions create friction and with each solution, you can scale and add zeros. My unique abilities help companies move through the process faster.

I take the clients' particular flywheel and remove one obstacle, freeing the flywheel to move more efficiently. We repeat the process over and over, and as you can imagine, every time we remove one obstacle this spinning flywheel moves faster and faster. Their techniques improve, business scales, and they never have to stop. Over time, they find themselves growing bigger and bigger. And as long as they never allow success to entertain complacency or conventional thinking, there is no limit to their reach and global impact.

This type of methodology allows you to take control of your life. You'll see your mindset changing bit by bit, and over time, your destiny will change. But better than that, you'll be so enthralled with your current status, you won't be worried about the end.

While others my age talk about retirement, I look for opportunity. Every day I wake up determined to provide value to someone. Each morning provides me a reset button to take what I did the day before and repeat or start over. This is the foundational principle of entrepreneurship.

Do you need assistance in building your natural curiosity, finding friction, or making connections? I invite you to visit my website and take the assessment to see if my unique ability can provide value to your entrepreneur journey. Adding zeros makes life an adventure—an adventure I will never finish because I'm not looking for a destination, I'm enjoying the journey. After all, better is infinite.

Stay Curious,

Chad

About The Author

Chad's zeal to understand how businesses work allows him to immediately understand and identify invisible opportunities in "the way we have always done it".

When Chad couples his three foundational elements–Apply the FILM, Just Add a Zero, and Growth through Collaboration–with his natural curiosity, these methods become the game-changer needed to move businesses toward exponential enterprise value growth.

This talent, what some call his highest value role, has opened the doors for Chad to work directly with leaders of businesses of every size across every industry. By analyzing the various aspects of an organization's friction, Chad can quickly identify invisible opportunities that enable companies to create competitive advantages and increase margins, resulting in exponential enterprise value growth. The result is a proven track record of over forty owned or previously owned high-growth companies and 100's of Growth Partnerships across North America.

Now focused on helping others, he has passed on leadership in each of his companies and operates solely in his Unique Ability through Growth Collaboration Partnerships and the SeedSpark Growth Academy.

Chad advises business leaders to stay curious and look for the friction in their own business to remove competition, name their price and go global through collaboration. If you need help Removing the Film, or Just Adding a Zero, contact Chad to discuss 100X Collaborations at www.SeedSpark.com.

Notes

Chapter 1

1. Clinton Nguyen. "7 World-Changing Inventions that Were Ridiculed When They Came Out." *Insider.* August 2, 2016. https://www.insider.com/inventions-that-were-ridiculed-2016-8.

2. Kary Oberbrunner. *Blockchain Life.* Powell, OH: Ethos, 2022.

3. Anil Bajnath. "Neuronal Plasticity: How Your Thoughts Literally Shape Your Brain." *The Institute for Human Optimization*, September 21, 2020. https://ifho.org/neuronal-plasticity-how-your-thoughts-literally-shape-your-brain/.

4. Jim Collins. *Good to Great: Why Some Companies Make the Leap...And Others Don't.* Harper Business, 2001.

Chapter 2

5. Jill Simonian. "8 Moms Who Used Motherhood to Reinvent Their Careers." *Parents.* February 10, 2023.

https://www.parents.com/parenting/work/moms-who-rei
nvented-their-careers-from-corporate-to-family-friendl
y/

6. Douglas Brackmann and Randy Kelley. *Driven: Understanding and Harnessing the Genetic Gifts Shared by Entrepreneurs, Navy SEALs, Pro Athletes, and Maybe YOU.* Lioncrest, 2017.

Chapter 3

7. Dan Sullivan "Who" reference goes here if needed. If not, numbers in the text from here forward will need to be adjusted.

Chapter 4

8. *Practical Psychology.* "9 Types of Intelligence – Howard Gardner." May 5, 2022. https://practicalpie.com/9-types-of-intelligence/.

9. Thomas Edison. "'Why, man, I have gotten a lot of results! I know several thousand things that won't work'...On my return, a few weeks later, his experiments had run up to over ten thousand..." In *Edison: His Life and Inventions (Illustrated)* by Frank Lewis Dyer and Thomas Commerford Martin. Green Booker Publishing, 1910. Kindle Edition.

Chapter 6

10. Serena Alagappan. "The Timeless Journey of the Möbius Strip." *Scientific American.* January 16, 2021. https://www.scientificamerican.com/article/the-timeless-journey-of-the-moebius-strip/.

11. Brett Berk. "Landau yachts: The history of Lincoln's Designer Series." *The AutoBlog.* February 6, 2022. https://www.autoblog.com/2022/02/06/lincoln-designer-series-history/.

Chapter 7

12. Roosevelt, Theodore. Theodore Roosevelt, An Autobiography. New York: Charles Scribner & Sons, 1913, p. 337.

CONNECT WITH CHAD

CHADTJENKINS.COM

SEEDSPARK
GROWTH ACADEMY

- Learn to Remove the Film

- Just Add a Zero

- Grow Exponentially
  Through Collaboration

GET STARTED AT
SEEDSPARK.COM

SEEDSPARK
GROWTH PARTNERS

Outperform your competition and *become a category of one.*

GET STARTED AT
SEEDSPARK.COM

WANT TO
ADD A ZER⭕?

Learn to remove the film,
outperform your competition,
and grow exponentially
through collaboration.

THIS BOOK IS PROTECTED INTELLECTUAL PROPERTY

The author of this book values Intellectual Property. The book you just read is protected by Easy IP™, a proprietary process, which integrates blockchain technology giving Intellectual Property "Global Protection." By creating a "Time-Stamped" smart contract that can never be tampered with or changed, we establish "First Use" that tracks back to the author.

Easy IP™ functions much like a Pre-Patent™ since it provides an immutable "First Use" of the Intellectual Property. This is achieved through our proprietary process of leveraging blockchain technology and smart contracts. As a result, proving "First Use" is simple through a global and verifiable smart contract. By protecting intellectual property with blockchain technology and smart contracts, we establish a "First to File" event.

Powered By Easy IP™

LEARN MORE AT EASYIP.TODAY

Made in the USA
Columbia, SC
19 November 2023